THE COMPLETE BOOK OF WATERSKIING

By Chris Boiling

WITH CONTRIBUTIONS FROM THE WORLD'S GREATEST SKIERS:
- **MIKE HAZELWOOD** MBE
- **SAMMY DUVALL**
- **RICKY McCORMICK**
- **KIM LASKOFF**
- **SCOTT CLACK**
- **MIKE SEIPEL**
- **STEVE MOORE** MBE

USEFUL ADDRESSES

This book is best used in conjunction with professional tuition. For a full list of ski schools and clubs in your area, contact your national federation:

AMERICAN WATER SKI ASSOCIATION, 799 Overlook Drive, Winter Haven, FL 33884 (Tel. 813 324 4341).

AUSTRALIAN WATER SKI ASSOCIATION, PO Box 211, South Melbourne 3205.

BRITISH WATER SKI FEDERATION, 390 City Road, London EC1V 2QA (Tel. 071 833 2855).

CANADIAN WATER SKI ASSOCIATION, 1600 James Naismith Drive, Gloucester, Ontario K1B 5N4 (Tel. 613 748 5683)

IRISH WATER SKI FEDERATION, c/o The Sports Council for NI, Upper Malone Road, Belfast BT9 5LA (0232 661 222).

NEW ZEALAND WATER SKI ASSOCIATION, PO Box 28 – 245, Rumuera, Auckland 5

SOUTH AFRICAN WATER SKI ASSOCIATION, PO Box 90177, Bertsham, Johannesburg 2013, South Africa

HAZELWOOD SKI CENTRE, 1217 North US Hwy 27, PO Box 338, Lake Hamilton, Florida, USA (Tel. 813 439 4754).

MIKE SEIPEL, Barefoot International, 2600 West Lantana Road, Lantana, Florida (Tel: 407 964 3346).

WATERSKI INTERNATIONAL, Europe's leading waterski magazine, Brinkworth House, Brinkworth, Nr Swindon, Wiltshire (Tel: 0666 41811).

British Library Cataloguing in Publication Data
Boiling, Christopher
  Complete book of waterskiing
  1. Water skiing
  I.Title
  797.35
  ISBN 0-340-52630-0

First published in 1991

© 1991 Christopher Boiling

Typeset by Tradespools Limited, Frome, Somerset
Printed for the educational publishing division of Hodder and Stoughton Ltd, Mill Road, Dunton Green, Sevenoaks, Kent by Colorcraft Ltd, Hong Kong

ACKNOWLEDGMENTS

Photographs by Tom King. Additional photographs by Chris Boiling and Gavin Newman, and courtesy of *Waterski International*, Cypress Gardens, Waterski Museum and Hall of Fame, British Disabled Water Ski Association/Oli Tennent, Yamaha Outboards.

The author and publishers would also like to thank all the skiers who contributed to this book and the following for their help: Carole Lowe, Jim Harmon, Jeremy Paxton, *Waterski International*, American Water Ski Association, British Water Ski Federation, Cypress Gardens.

CONTENTS

WATERSKIING
FOR FUN

INTRODUCTION

The most popular form of waterskiing – slalom skiing.

It's easy to become hooked on waterskiing. The sense of freedom as you skim across the surface of the water, the speed and power you can generate by simply pulling a rope, the challenge of learning the next step – these are all addictive.

But in this book we will teach you more than how to waterski. We will teach you how to soar 200 feet through the air, how to kick up huge walls of spray, how to do spectacular somersaults, how to race at more than 80 m.p.h., how to ski without skis, and how to become a world champion. The direction you choose to go in is up to you. That is the great thing about this fast-growing family sport – there is so much variety.

The father of waterskiing – Ralph Samuelson.

Waterskiing has certainly come a long way since 18-year-old Ralph Samuelson unwittingly invented the sport in the summer of 1922. A fun-loving adventurer, Samuelson used to enjoy being dragged round Lake Pepin at Lake City, Minnesota, USA, riding on a large, flat board being pulled by his brother Ben's 24 ft work launch. He also used to slide down the snowy banks of the lake on barrel staves. Then he tried to use these on the lake, without much success. So he tried it again using 7 ft snow skis. But he soon realised he needed skis with a larger surface area, especially since his brother's boat, powered by a converted Saxon truck engine, only had a top speed of 20 m.p.h.

Samuelson went out and bought two pine boards for a dollar each from a lumber yard and cut them down so they measured 8 feet long by 9 inches wide. He softened one end of each plank by steaming it, then curled up the edges by clamping them in a vice. With the help of his sister, Harriet, he painted them white, and from a harness shop, he bought some scrap leather and made binders for his feet. To complete his equipment he bought 100 feet of sash cord from a local hardware store and got an iron ring from a blacksmith. He put black tape all the way round it and this was his handle.

With this primitive equipment, and with no knowledge to help him, he took five days to get up. At first he tried stepping off his large, flat board, but didn't get very far. He tried without the board, first with his skis level and then with the tips in the water. Then on Sunday, 2 July he had an idea – he pushed back on his skis and kept the tips out of the water. A new sport was born and skiers have been using this start method ever since. What a way to celebrate his 19th birthday the next day! As well as being the first waterskier, Samuelson was also the first waterski jumper. He began by jumping wakes – cracking his first pair of skis after landing from a particularly big wave. For his next pair, he reinforced the tips and moved the straps back – this is the pair pictured here, now on display in the Waterski Museum and Hall of Fame in Winter Haven, Florida.

Samuelson demonstrated his skills all over Minnesota, jumping from a 4 ft × 16 ft diving platform, converted into a jump ramp by removing the floating supports from one end. His first attempt was at Lake Pepin on 8 July, 1925, but, like many skiers before and since, he came off the

Samuelson's skis at the Waterski Museum and Hall of Fame, Winter Haven, Florida.

5 ft end head first. In this case, the skis had stuck to the 30-degree incline. Lard was put on the ramp surface for his next attempt and he succeeded. Later that summer, he became the first speed skier – by skiing successfully behind Walter Bullock's WW1-vintage Curtiss flying boat. His speed was recorded at 80 m.p.h. Again, his first attempt was a flop. The plane was going at about 60 m.p.h. when it began to bounce on the water – Bullock, one of Northwest Airline's first pilots, had planned to fly a few feet above it. But the unsuccessful attempt to take

Ralph Samuelson's 'death-defying ride' behind Walter Bullock's World War I vintage Curtiss flying boat.

off jerked Samuelson out of his skis and onto his stomach. 'My first thought wasn't for my safety, but whether I'd lost my swimming suit,' he told biographer, Gregor Ziemer. Next time he was lucky, with an estimated 2000 people witnessing as advertised his 'death-defying ride on water . . . behind a flying boat.'

Samuelson at the peak of his stunt skiing career.

That same year, on 22 August, 1925, a 38-year-old inventor from Long Island, New York, patented a pair of Dolphin Akwar-Skees. Fred Waller, a keen sportsman, had tested the 8 ft Skees himself in Long Island Sound and was able to perform tricks with them. The Skees were similar to today's trainer skis, in that the skier held onto ropes coming from the tips of the skis rather than directly from the boat, and the boat actually pulled the mahogany Skees, via a Y-shaped rope connected with a bridle, rather than directly pulling the skier. Waller went on to produce more than 50 inventions, including Cinerama, and when he died in 1954 most Americans considered him to be the father of waterskiing.

Meanwhile, Samuelson had introduced waterskiing to other places: to Detroit, when he went to work for the Ford Motor Company, and to Florida, when he went to work in a boat livery – skiing during the intervals at speedboat races. During one show a large wake knocked off one of his skis – he finished on the other one and introduced slalom skiing into his act! Tourists visiting Florida, especially the French, are believed to have taken the idea home with them and developed the sport on the Riviera.

Samuelson's skiing career ended suddenly in March 1927 when he broke his back in an accident at the Palm Beach boat business where he worked. Depressed, he returned to Lake City with his skis and put them in the attic of his family's boathouse. They reappeared in the 1950s, long after Samuelson had left Lake City, on the wall of the city's new bathhouse. Under them was a hand-written placard which read: 'The World's First Water Skis'.

But the story behind them may have remained a secret to the outside world had not an inquisitive reporter gone on holiday there. Margaret Mason (née Crimmins), who worked for the St Paul *Pioneer Press Dispatch*, wandered into the bathhouse and spotted the skis in the summer of 1963. She asked the waterfront supervisor, a man called Ben Simons, about them. He had seen Samuelson's first attempts and had preserved the skis for history, but hadn't seen Samuelson for about 15 years. Mason wrote an article in her paper asking: 'Where are you now, Mr Samuelson? I wish I knew. So do Simons and a lot of other Lake Cityites who are proud of their native son.' Samuelson was living about 30 miles away with his second wife when a local storekeeper reported that someone was looking for him. He went to St Paul with scrapbooks full of old clippings and photos and told Mason his story. Nothing much happened after it was published but a second one in 1965 attracted the attention of the American Water Ski Association, who had proclaimed Fred Waller as the sport's inventor.

In February 1966 the Association announced that Samuelson was the official Father of Waterskiing. Eleven years later, in August 1977, he died of cancer. But his sport is now enjoyed by more than 20 million people all over the world. There are world champions in all the disciplines – tournament (slalom, tricks and jump), barefoot, racing and freestyle. In this book, the top skiers of today pass on their knowledge to the champions of tomorrow. But to get to the top you have to start at the bottom, with the basics. Learn them well and you will have a solid foundation for your climb to the pinnacle of this exhilarating and most photogenic of sports.

Cory Pickos performs one of his many spectacular tricks.
Left: *How skis have changed in forty years. Susi Graham with a ski from the 1950s and her modern slalom ski.*

1 LEARNING TO SKI

Waterskiing is easy. It is something that almost anyone can do, whether six and under, or 70 and over. If Ralph Samuelson could do it on a pair of $1 pine boards, measuring 8 ft long by 9 ins wide, and pulled by a 24 ft, 24 h.p. inboard that could only go about 20 m.p.h, you can surely do it with today's designer skis and powerful, purpose-built boats. But, beware, once you try it you are likely to become addicted . . .

The first hurdle to overcome is 'getting up'. Few people can do it first time but it is possible if you remember:

● to start in the correct position (see photo);

● to keep your arms straight and your knees bent;

● to let the boat pull you out of the water (if you try to pull yourself up, you will end up learning another sport – swimming).

Before you get into the water to learn this 'deepwater start', practise it on land so you have a clear idea of what to do. Here are the six simple steps to getting up and skiing away first time.

1 The first thing to do is to put your skis on. It is easier if both your feet and the rubber bindings on the skis are wet, so dip your feet and the ski bindings in water first. Then slide your toes in the bindings and pull up the rubber heel. The bindings should feel comfortable and snug – neither tight nor loose.

2 Once you have the skis fitted, sit down on them – bend your knees and sit behind the bindings. Tuck your knees up to your chest and make sure the skis are fairly close together.

3 Hold the handle as shown, with your knuckles on top. This is the overhand grip.

4 Stretch your arms out in front of you.

5 Have someone (preferably an experienced skier or professional coach) pull you up gradually with the towline.

6 Use your legs to stand up, don't pull yourself up with your arms.

Once you have done this a few times you are ready for the real thing. Put on a life jacket. As well as being an essential for safety, it will help you float without wasting energy. Float in the sitting position you have just learned on land, with your knees up against your chest, the tips of the skis just out of the water and your arms straight across the outside of your knees. Your knees should be just out of the water; the skis about shoulder width apart. The towline should be between your skis so you get a straight pull from the boat and the handle just below the surface of the water. Stay in this position until the towline is taut. If you lose your balance, let go with one arm and paddle back into position.

Relax. When you are in the correct position and the line is taut, shout 'Hit it'. ('Go' can be confused with 'No' or 'Wow' and *vice versa*.) This is the signal for the boat driver to accelerate smoothly and quickly and pull you out of the water. Remember, the boat does most of the work. You should just be concentrating on keeping your arms straight, your legs bent and on not trying to pull yourself up. Try to keep the skis close together as well. If they drift apart, you could end up doing the splits!

The time for you to stand up is when you have broken the surface of the water and are already gliding along. Don't rush to stand up or you will push the tips of the skis under the water and fall flat on your face. To stand up, rock slightly forward, transferring your weight from the heels so that it is evenly distributed over your foot, and push up slowly with your legs. The boat will do the rest. When you are up, just follow the boat round and gain confidence. Think about your body position: keep your arms straight, knees bent, back straight, head up and skis about shoulder width apart. And still try to relax. If the water becomes rougher, or another boat creates some wash, just bend your knees to absorb the shock.

The correct skiing position.

Many beginners ski with their backside sticking out, which looks hilarious and is very uncomfortable. If this is you, try to push your hips forward, your shoulders up and back, and keep your head up in the 'proud' position.

CROSSING THE WAKES

When you have got the feel for skiing and are confident behind the boat, it is time to start turning and crossing the wakes, the waves created by the boat. This will probably be lesson two or three.

Get the feel of going one way then the other, by skiing from side to side between the wakes. To do this, just put a little more weight on the right ski to go to the right and on the left to go to the left. At the same time, push forward lightly with the other ski, just as snow skiers do. As you build confidence, push a bit harder on the outside ski. This will put your skis more on 'edge' and make your turns tighter. Now ski across the wakes. Be bold, be aggressive – you are more likely to fall if you are timid and cautious. Shift your weight and push on the outside ski, edging towards the wake, and all the way through it. When the skis are on edge they will cut right through the wake, not bounce off it. Keep your knees bent to absorb the turbulence.

To return to the centre, push hard on the outside ski and shift a little weight to the inside ski. Cut through the wake. When you are through the wash you can straighten up and follow the boat again, evening out the distribution of your weight. When you are ready, cut through the opposite wake. Then be bold and go through both wakes without pausing in between.

After a while – and a few falls – you will be skiing from side to side with ease and experiencing the great thrill of skiing wide of the boat. Don't be frightened or embarrassed about falling – it's all part of the learning process. Although, if you are going to fall, try to fall backwards or to the side, rather than forward.

STOPPING

When you are tired or your time is up, signal that you want to head back to the jetty/dock/beach/landing area (see chapter 15 for a description of all hand signals). However, don't head straight for the dock – you may misjudge your speed and crash into it. Approach the area parallel to it, drop the handle to one side and gently glide until you sink close to the jetty. The more experienced you become, the closer you will get. If you find yourself heading for danger or are coming in too fast, sit back, cup your hands and drag them in the water. If you are still heading for disaster, fall.

EQUIPMENT FOR BEGINNERS

- A pair of skis – the size will depend on the weight of the skier (larger skis for larger people). These skis – either wooden or made from a modern fibreglass combination – should have adjustable bindings.
- A lifejacket/ski vest – the three- and four-buckle varieties are best for skiing.
- A boat – it has to be powerful enough to pull you out of the water (and should have power to spare).
- A driver and observer – the observer keeps an eye on the skier and relays his signals to the driver.
- A tow rope with a handle. The standard length of this is 75 ft.
- A wetsuit or drysuit – these will help keep cold-water skiers warm. (A wetsuit lets a little water in but this is soon warmed by the body; a drysuit keeps the water out but is more cumbersome.)

Shifting weight to the inside ski to cut back towards the wake.

2 MONO SKIING

14

One ski is more manoeuvrable than two, so you can turn more sharply and kick up more spray.

Traversing from side to side is the basic manoeuvre in slalom skiing, the most popular form of waterskiing. But in slalom skiing it is done on one ski.

Forty-five years ago skiers went round six buoys in a straight line on two skis. Now they go around three buoys 11.5 m to the left of the centre and another three 11.5 m to the right – on one ski. So you have got to learn to 'drop a ski' and mono ski. That is the next hurdle for you to overcome.

Skiing on one ski is not difficult, and you will be able to turn much sharper and have more fun. Kicking up a great wall of spray is one of the most thrilling and beautiful sights around. The first thing to do on the road to this goal is decide which foot is going to go in front of the other on your slalom ski.

There are two ways to decide this. The first is to stand with your feet together on land and fall forward. The foot which naturally steps forward to prevent you falling should be your front foot on the slalom ski. A better way of deciding is to ski behind a boat on a pair of skis and to slowly transfer all your weight on to one ski and lift the other one clear of the water. Do it only once, then slowly put all your weight on the opposite leg and again try to lift the other ski. Whichever one feels stronger and you are able to balance better on, that will be your forward leg. Now practise lifting a ski and riding on your forward leg. This is known as the *skier's salute*.

While you are lifting a ski, resist the temptation to bend your back – keep it straight so that the only part of your body moving is your leg. Remember, too, to keep the tip of the ski well clear of the water and to transfer your weight and lift your leg slowly. There is no rush: the World Waterski Championships only come around every two years.

The skier's salute.

Two other points:
● Don't look down at the water;
● Keep your standing leg bent.

Hold the ski out of the water for as long as you can. As soon as you start wobbling, put it back in the water, then lift it again. When you can lift it indefinitely, it is time to learn to drop it. The first thing to do when dropping a ski is to make sure that the binding on the ski to be dropped is loose. Then go through the following steps on land before you try it in the water. Having a clear idea of what you have to do will save a few falls.

1 Shift your weight on to the skiing leg.

2 Maintain good body position, e.g. back straight, head up, skiing leg slightly bent.

3 Slowly ease your foot out of the binding, brush the ski backwards, and lift your foot up. The water will carry the ski away.

Dropping a ski.

4 Lift the foot clear of the spray, to where it was when you were lifting a ski.

5 Stay relaxed. If you feel you are losing your balance, put your free foot in the water with your toes pointed down. Stay in this position until you have regained your balance. Then lift your foot again.

6 Now put your free foot behind the knee of your skiing leg.

7 Slowly slide the foot down the back of the skiing leg and on to the ski behind the front binding. Do not rush to put your free foot in the rear binding, just rest it lightly on the ski and ski along with it that way for a while. Sliding the foot down the back of the skiing leg makes it easier to find the rear binding and keep the foot out of the spray. Many learners fall, not when they drop the ski but as they try (in vain) to find the back binding.

8 When you are comfortable, riding along with the rear foot just resting on the ski, gradually work it back over the top of the rear toe loop and then into it. Do everything slowly so you don't lose your balance.

9 Gradually increase the pressure on your rear foot until it is flat, your knees are together and your weight is evenly distributed.

10 Check your body position. Your knees should be bent, your back should be straight and your arms should be pulled down towards the hips and have a slight kink in them. Keep the knees together so that the legs work as one unit. Bend the knees more as you cross the wakes or reach rough water. If you are finding it hard to keep your knees close together, check the distance between the tips of your back foot toes and the heel of your front foot – they should be less than an inch (2.5 cm) apart.

Mike Hazelwood demonstrates the correct body position when crossing the wakes.

The amount of bend in the knees will vary, as you cross the wake or reach rough water – remember, your knees are your shock absorbers. The rest of your body must be straight, with your hips pushed as far forward as possible. This position may feel a little strange at first but now is the time to get into good habits – bad habits are often hard to break and will slow up your progress. Whatever you do, resist the temptation to break at the waist (bend forward).

CROSSING THE WAKES

Once you are skiing steadily on one ski, the next step is to cross the wake. Do not view the wake as a huge obstacle – with the correct body position, it is an easy thing to tackle. Maintaining the correct body position is the key to success.

First, just drift from one side of the wake to the other. Don't go out too far. Once you can do this maintaining the correct body position, move about 10 metres outside the wake. Then slowly begin to turn your head and shoulders to the opposite side (at a 60 degree angle). Keep the ski on edge through both wakes so that it cuts through them and does not bounce across. As with two skis, be bold – don't hesitate. Stop edging or cutting when you are clear of the second wake. This will slow you down, so you can start to turn by changing edge. Do this six to eight times in a row, always maintaining that vital, all-important body position. This is the basis of slalom skiing. Once you reach this stage you will be feeling really good: confident and enjoying this great sport even more.

BASEBALL GRIP

Now is the time to get used to holding the handle with one hand on top and the other underneath – the *baseball grip*. There is no hard and fast rule about which hand should be palm up and which palm down – the pros are split about 50/50. However, the general consensus is that there is a slight advantage for right foot forward skiers to have their right hand on top, and for left foot forward skiers to have their left hand on top – in this way supporting their weak side turns. Right palm down, left palm up will help on buoys 1, 3 and 5, which are normally a right foot forward skier's weakest turns. Left palm down, right palm up will help on buoys 2, 4 and 6, which are normally a left foot forward skier's weakest turns.

The baseball grip.

3 ONE-SKI STARTS

Camille Duvall demonstrates the correct position to get into for a deepwater start.

The deepwater start on one ski is considered by many to be one of the hardest parts of waterskiing. Others get the hang of it straight away, and it need not be a difficult hurdle to get over if you remember a few basic tips:

1 Get in the correct position. Your forward foot should be in the binding. Bring your knee into your chest, as you did when you were learning on two skis, and keep the ski tip out of the water (6–10 inches). The free leg will be behind you, acting like a rudder. When the boat starts pulling you out of the water, use your free leg to keep your balance. Wear an approved flotation aid to help you to keep afloat.

2 With your weight distributed evenly over the ski, remember to keep your shoulders square to the boat, arms slightly bent and head up. (Keeping your head up will arch your back and help you get out of the water.)

3 Keep your hands and the handle close to your ankle.

4 The ski rope should be on the inside of the ski (to the left of the ski if your left leg is your free leg).

5 Resist the temptation to stand up too fast – you will be pulled over the front of the ski. You can only stand up successfully when the ski is moving fast enough to support your body.

6 As you come out of the water, move your shoulders back but keep your back straight. Don't rush to stand up. Once you are up, you can put your rear foot in the binding.

Those preferring to start with both feet in the binding should make sure that the ski is as flat as possible with the tip only two to three inches out of the water. As the boat begins to accelerate, keep your weight on your front foot, allowing the ski to stay flat, and plane as quickly as it can. Heavier skies starting with two feet in the bindings may struggle to get up if the boat is underpowered because of the extra drag created by this start method.

Deepwater start.

SITTING DOCK START

A useful start method to learn before the weather and water turn colder is the sitting dock start – it will keep you dry above the knees. The procedure is more or less the same whether you have one or two skis on, but by now you should be comfortable mono skiing.

1 Put your ski on before you sit down.

2 Sit down on the edge of the dock with the tail of your ski under the water and the tip a couple of inches out of it. The ski should be at an angle of about 30 degrees.

3 You should be facing the back of the boat with your free foot hanging loose to the side, ready to help you keep balance.

4 Keep your arms close to your body and the handle in to your stomach. Lean back slightly with your upper body.

Sitting dock start.

5 Shout 'hit it' and let the boat pull you off the dock.

6 Resist the pull of the boat, don't let it jerk you forward. Don't anticipate the pull either – this will lead to the ski sinking and you being pulled forward and getting wet unnecessarily.

BEACH/SCOOTER START

Wade into the water until it comes nearly up to your knees. Your ski should be on your front foot. Stand on your free foot and lift your ski out in front of you. Keep the tip out of the water and the tail under. Your weight should be over the ski, so you will have to drop your shoulder over your skiing leg.

Beach start.

Your knees, back and arms should be bent to take the pull of the boat. Hold the handle on the same side as the ski. The other hand should be holding a couple of coils of the rope loosely. Be careful to ensure that none of your fingers will be trapped when the boat begins to pull. As the last coil unwinds, grab hold of the handle with both hands and prepare to resist the pull. Use your free foot for balance and, again, don't anticipate the pull of the boat unless you want to go swimming!

STANDING DOCK START

When you are ready to pose, this is the start for you.

Stand on the edge of the dock, holding the front of your ski up and a couple of coils of rope in your hand. Let the boat pull you off. As it does so, push your ski out in front of you. The main thing with this start is the timing between you and the boat driver.

Standing dock start – it's the same principles whether you are on one ski or two skis, slalom, trick or jump skis.

20

EQUIPMENT

'Try before you buy' is the best advice when selecting equipment such as boats and skis. Generally, you get the quality you pay for, but buying the most expensive ski may not help your skiing. The top-of-the-range skis are only meant for the most advanced skiers, who can take advantage of a ski which is designed to be ridden aggressively on a short line.

All you really need to go skiing – a good boat, skis, rope, wetsuit and buoyancy aid.

The essential equipment for waterskiers is a powerful boat, ski or skis, rope and handle and lifejacket. In colder climes it is also advisable to have a wetsuit to keep you warm. When you are learning it is easy and advisable to hire or borrow equipment until you have more knowledge of the sport and know exactly what boat and ski(s) will best suit your needs.

A good ski boat is one which has the power to pull the heaviest skier up on a deepwater mono ski start (even with two feet in the bindings), makes little or no wakes at slalom and jump speeds, produces crisp, even and high wakes at trick speeds, can accelerate quickly up to 36 m.p.h., will hold its course even when a strong skier is trying to pull it from side to side, has a rear-facing observer's seat, a rear-view mirror, and plenty of storage space for skis and other equipment. Other considerations include length and weight (will you need to tow the boat behind your car?) and where you are going to go skiing (lake or sea?) There are many purpose-built ski boats which are best for the job but because of their hull design (they are relatively flat bottomed) they are not suited to coastal skiing where a deeper v-shaped hull is better suited for cutting through the waves.

The leading ski boat manufacturers are Correct Craft and MasterCraft. Supra, Ski Supreme, Malibu and American Skier also produce sought after ski boats. In Britain, Craig Craft challenges the market leaders and in Australia, Flightcraft pulls the major championships. In Continental Europe, Boesch is among the leading brands. Sports boat eminently suitable for recreational skiers include models from Fletcher International, Sunbird, Shakespeare, Bayliner, Four Winns, Phantom, Ring, Picton, Plancraft, Spirit, Donzi, Renken, Rinker, Sea Ray, and Maxum.

Ski boats should have a sturdy ski pole and rear-facing seat for the observer.

As well as there being a huge variety of boats to choose from, there is also a huge range of engine options. Apart from power and brand, there are basically three types to choose from: outboard, stern drive (inboard/outdrive), and inboards.

Outboards have the advantage that they are separate from the hull, so you can replace or upgrade them when you need to and they are easy to remove for servicing. Also, because they are fixed to the outside of the transom (back of the boat), they do not take up any room inside the boat. Unlike inboard and stern drive engines, outboards are not derived from car engines, so maintenance may be a little more difficult, but because they have been designed purely with boats in mind, they pack a lot of power into a relatively small amount of space. They vary in power from 2 to 250 h.p., with 25 h.p. the minimum for waterskiing – 75–90 h.p. is more common for serious recreational skiers. The handling is often less balanced than with other engine configurations and you will need to use the trim for optimum performance. Outboards can be tilted up and down to protect the propeller when launching and recovering the boat.

22

Leading brand names include Mercury, Mariner, Johnson, Evinrude, Suzuki, Yamaha and Force.

Ninety per cent of family boats are stern drives, which have the engine mounted inside the boat with an outdrive unit going through the transom to provide the power and steering. They are said to combine the best attributes of inboards and outboards. Like inboards, stern drives are generally marinised car engines, (i.e. adapted so that they can work in a marine environment), so they are easy to maintain if you are familiar with auto engines. Like outboards, you can trim the engine to regulate the ride, and tilt it to aid launching and recovery. Handling is easy provided that the boat is fitted with power steering.

Companies providing stern drive power plants include Volvo Penta, Mercruiser, OMC Cobra, and Yamaha.

Most competition ski boats are inboards. Skiers like the powerful pull out of the hole and drivers enjoy the stable handling characteristics which come from placing a large marinised auto engine in the centre of the boat. This combined with a centre-mounted pylon make it hard for the skier to pull the boat off course. The flat-bottomed hull design means that the boat will plane fast, but is very stable; that it tracks well, leaves a consistent wake, and does not bank in the turn. Disadvantages include a hard ride in choppy waters, less room for passengers and, because the propeller is under the hull, it is difficult to launch an inboard boat in shallow water and at the coast.

The main inboard engine suppliers are Chrysler Marine, Pleasurecraft Marine, Mercury Marine, Indmar and Commander.

SKIS

The development of skis took a quantum leap forward in the late 1960s/early 1970s when fibreglass started to replace wood as the main material used in the manufacture of skis. Wooden skis are still available for beginners and racers but tend not to last as long as their hi-tech counterparts. Usually the first skis a skier buys is a 'combi' pair, which can be used by someone learning on two skis and also later on by someone learning to mono ski because one of the pair has been set up for slalom skiing: it has a rear toe piece and a deep fin (metal is better than plastic). The bigger the skier, the bigger the ski he will need. Basically, skiers over 11 stone will need a 67 or 68-inch ski, very large skiers might need as much as a 72-inch ski. Medium-sized skiers of nine to 11 stone will need about a 65–66 inch ski. Smaller skiers will need 63–64-inch skis. As skiers improve, they may be able to ski on shorter skis. As a rough guide, the ski should come up to about nose height on a skier.

Generally with skis, you get what you pay for, but very few skiers will ever reach the level where they can benefit from all the fine design features of the very expensive 'pro' skis at the top of each manufacturers' range. Many of the mid-range skis are excellent for intermediate level slalom skiers. In fact, many of these skis were top-of-the-range skis a few years ago. If possible, try a ski before you buy.

As important as getting a good quality ski is making sure that the binding is of good quality, i.e. strong and comfortable. A binding should give firm support at the ankle but give quick release to the foot or feet in a fall.

As mentioned earlier, good metal fins are preferred to plastic which break easily, but only the experts need aerofoils or wings on their fins. These help the skier slow down quicker and are essential for shortline slalom. By the time you come to choose jump, trick or racing skis, you will probably know exactly what you want, or know enough other skiers to be able to try some different makes before you buy. The leading brand names are O'Brien, Kidder, Jobe, Connelly, EP, HO and Cypress Gardens. Fred Williams and Ron Marks skis are big in Australia; Reflex are big in France.

LIFEJACKET

There are many good lifejackets and specially designed ski vests on the market which will provide protection in the event of a fall and help to keep you afloat while doing deepwater starts. It is essential that they are a good fit and do not ride up in the water. Three- and four-buckle vests are best for skiing.

TOWLINE

For normal recreational skiing a *polypropylene line* is ideal, either 23 m (75 ft) or 18.25 m (60 ft). You won't need a line with colourful shortenings marked off until you get into shortline slalom skiing. A shorter line will be needed for tricks and an extra long one – say, 40–45 m – will be used for racing.

HANDLES

A good quality wooden handle is recommended. Special handles are available for tricks and barefoot, and twin handles are used in racing.

WETSUIT/DRYSUIT

Wetsuits and drysuits not only keep you warm but also offer sensitive areas protection against water pressure injuries. Thinner summer and thicker winter wetsuits are available. They should be a good fit and not restrict movement.

GLOVES

Gloves can improve grip and help prevent blisters.

HELMETS

Helmets are essential for jumpers and racers. Only buy helmets that are approved for your chosen discipline.

- DON'T BE IN A HURRY
- TALK TO OTHER SKIERS
- VISIT SEVERAL CLUBS AND STOCKISTS
- TRY BEFORE YOU BUY, IF POSSIBLE

24

When we say wear a suit, we mean a wetsuit or drysuit.

2

WATERSKIING WITH THE CHAMPIONS

5 TOURNAMENT SKIING

The classic form of competitive waterskiing is called *tournament*, as opposed to barefoot and racing. Tournament waterskiing is made up of three completely different events – slalom, tricks (figures) and jumping. All require different skills and all have something different to offer the spectator.

- Slalom is fast and rhythmic with the skier using all his/her strength to beat the boat and course.
- Tricks, or figures as some people call it, combines elements of figure skating and gymnastics.
- Jumping is the most spectacular event, offering the magic combination of speed and possible spills.

Skiers who compete in all three events can win the most prestigious title, that of overall champion. The following formulae are used to equate the performances from each event:

TRICKS AND SLALOM $\dfrac{\text{Skier's score}}{\text{Winner's score}} \times 1000$

(NB. Slalom score = No. of consecutive buoys scored from start speed.)

MEN'S JUMP $\dfrac{\text{Skier's score} - 10\,\text{m}}{\text{Winner's score} - 10\,\text{m}} \times 1000$

WOMEN'S JUMP $\dfrac{\text{Skier's score} - 7\,\text{m}}{\text{Winner's score} - 7\,\text{m}} \times 1000$

Basically, the winner of each event gets 1,000 points and the other skiers get a proportion of 1,000 points based on their score in relation to that of the winner. The person with the most points becomes the overall champion. Anybody winning slalom, tricks and jump would score 3,000 points. But, usually, the overall champions are very strong in one or two events and competent in the third.

Line length Metric	Imperial	Distance off	Colour of rope	Extra room	Score at this stage
22.9 m	75 ft	long line		38 ft	
18.25 m	60 ft	15 off	red	22 ft	6 @ 18.25 m = 6 @ 15 off = 24 buoys
16 m	52 ft	22	orange	15 ft	6 @ 16 m = 6 @ 22 off = 30 buoys
14.25 m	47 ft	28	yellow	9 ft	6 @ 14.25 m = 6 @ 28 off = 36 buoys
13 m	43 ft	32	green	5 ft	6 @ 13 m = 6 @ 32 off = 42 buoys
12 m	39 ft	35	blue	2 ft	6 @ 12 m = 6 @ 35 off = 48 buoys
11.25 m	37 ft	38	violet (blue/white)	− 1 ft	6 @ 11.25 m = 6 @ 38 off = 54 buoys
10.75 m	35 ft	39½	white	− 2½ ft	6 @ 10.75 m = 6 @ 39½ off = 60 buoys

SLALOM

The diagram below shows the layout of the slalom course. The tow boat is driven down the centre of the course between a line of guide buoys. The skier enters the course through a set of two of these guide buoys (known as the entrance gate), skis around six turning buoys (three to the right and three to the left), and exits through two more guide buoys (the exit gate). The boat then turns around and comes back through the course again; the exit gate now becoming the entrance gate.

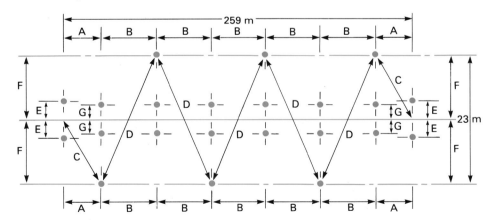

DIMENSIONS

259 m OVERALL:

A = 27 m
B = 41 m   TOLERANCES:
C = 29.347 m ±¼% on 259 m
D = 47.011 m ± ½% on A, B, C, D
E = 1.25 m   ± 1% on F
F = 11.5 m   ± 5% on E
G = 1.15 m   ± 10% on G

ALLOWED RANGES ON DIMENSIONS

258.353 m − 259.648 m
26.865 m − 27.135 m
40.795 m − 41.205 m
29.200 m − 29.494 m
46.776 m − 47.246 m
1.188 m − 1.313 m
11.385 m − 11.615 m
1.035 m − 1.265 m

Note: The average of the six measured F dimensions cannot be less than 11.48 m.
Not to scale.

Official slalom course

The skier carries on skiing until he/she misses a buoy or falls. Each successive trip (called a pass) through the course is made more difficult for the skier by increasing the speed in 3 k.p.h. increments for each pass until a maximum boat speed is achieved (58 k.p.h./36 m.p.h. for men and 55 k.p.h/34 m.p.h. for women). Once a skier can ski the course at the maximum speed, the rope is shortened by predetermined lengths on each pass: from 18.25 m to 16 m, then 14.25 m, 13 m, 12 m, 11.25 m, 10.75 m and finally 10.25 m (the world record shortening). (In America, skiers don't refer to the actual rope length in metres, they talk about the number of feet off the standard 75 ft rope length. So, 12 m is known as 35 off, 11.25 m is 38 off and 10.75 m is 39.5 off.) Some ropes come with different coloured sections, so it is easy for judges and observers to see what line length the skier is on. For example, 12 m is blue, 11.25 m is pink and 10.75 m is white.

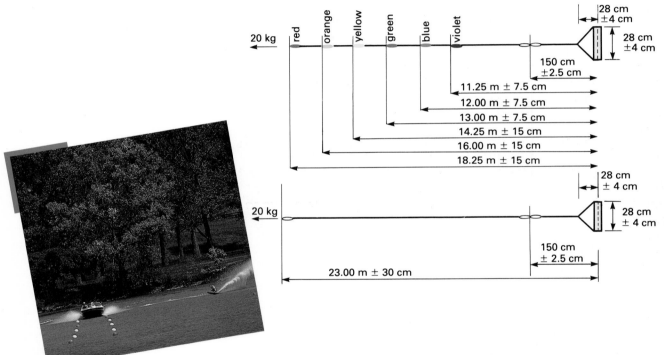

The winner is the skier who successfully negotiates the most buoys at the shortest rope length, or who achieves the highest number of consecutive buoys. Because of the physical demands required to negotiate a slalom pass, skiers will normally elect to start their events at a boat speed and rope length equivalent to about four passes before they expect to fall or miss. As soon as they successfully complete their first pass, they will score all the buoys they opted to ignore. If they fail to complete their first pass, they will only get the points for the buoys rounded in that pass – and none for the ones they skipped.

When a skier falls or misses a buoy, he will be credited with a full buoy, half buoy or quarter buoy (no three-quarter buoy), depending upon where the fall or miss occurred. A full buoy is scored when the skier rounds the turning buoy and gets back to the boat's wake (middle of the course). A half buoy is scored when the skier gets around the turning buoy but does not make it to the boat's wake. A quarter buoy means the skier makes it past the turning buoy in a skiing position but fails to turn around it.

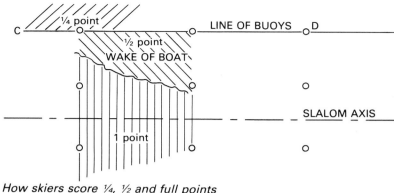

How skiers score ¼, ½ and full points

The boat speed has to be the same for each skier, so the boat is timed between various buoys to a 100th of a second. At 36 m.p.h., the boat should take 16.08 seconds to go through the course. If the boat is out of tolerance (i.e. not between 15.93 and 16.23 secs), a re-ride is given. If the boat was too fast, making the pass more difficult than it should have been, the skier is given an optional re-ride. If the boat was too slow, he is given a mandatory re-ride.

Although the boat speed remains constant through the course, the skier's speed is anything but constant. He or she is continually accelerating and decelerating to reach the buoys and then round them. To turn, the skier needs to slow down to 10–20 m.p.h. (16–32 km/h), but to reach the next buoy in time he or she must accelerate up to speeds of 60–70 m.p.h. (96–112 km/h) – all in the space of a second or two. The tension on the towline at these speeds is tremendous. At times, skiers must hold on to forces that are three to five times their own weight. Pull tests have shown that the top men skiers approach 1,000 pounds of pull at times.

TRICKS

Official trick course

Balance and athletic agility are the keys to trick skiing. Each trick has a different point value based upon its degree of difficulty. The more difficult, high-scoring tricks include front and back flips, bodyovers (where a skier jumps over the towline), 900-degree turns and toeholds (where the rope is attached to the skier's foot). Skiers try to do as many high-scoring tricks as possible, without repetition, in two 20-second passes, or before they fall, whichever is soonest. A panel of five judges, watching from the side of the lake/river, credit the trick if it is performed correctly.

There are no points for style, but the 'cleaner' a trick is performed, the easier it is for the judges to score it. The top trick skiers, like Cory Pickos and Patrice Martin, can score over 10,000 points – more than a trick a second. The top women – such as Tawn Larsen and Natalia Rumiantseva – can score over 8,000 points.

Unlike the other disciplines, trick skiers are allowed to select their own boat speed and rope length.

SURFACE TURNS						
			2 skis		1 ski	
Code	Description	No.	Bas	Rev	Bas	Rev
S	Side slide	1	20	20	40	40
TS	Toehold side slide	2	—	—	130	130
B	180 F–B	3	30	30	60	60
F	B–F	4	30	30	60	60
O	360 F–F	5	40	40	90	90
BB	B–B		40	40	90	90
5B	540 F–B		50	—	110	—
5F	B–F		50	—	110	—
7F	720 F–F		60	—	130	—
7B	B–B		60	—	130	—
LB	180 F–B Stepover	6	70	70	110	—
LF	B–F Stepover	7	70	70	110	—
TB	180 F–B Toehold	8	—	—	100	100
TF	B–F Toehold	9	—	—	100	100
TO	360 F–F Toehold	10	—	—	200	200
TBB	B–B Toehold	11	—	—	200	200
T5B	540 F–B Toehold	12	—	—	350	350
T7F	720 F–F Toehold		—	—	450	—
T5F	540 B–F Toehold	13	—	—	350	—

WAKE TURNS						
			2 skis		1 ski	
Code	Description	No.	Bas	Rev	Bas	Rev
WB	180 F–F	14	50	50	80	80
WF	B–F	15	50	50	80	80
WO	360 F–F	16	110	110	150	150
WBB	B–B	17	110	110	150	150
W5B	540 F–B	18	310	310	310	310
W5F	B–F	19	310	310	310	310
W7F	720 F–F	20	600	600	600	600
W7B	B–B	21	480	480	480	480
W9B	900 F–B	22	700	700	700	700
W9F	B–F		700	700	700	700
WLB	180 F–B Stepover	23	110	110	160	—
WLF	B–F Stepover	24	110	110	160	—
WLO	360 F–F Stepover	25	200	200	260	260
WLBB	B–B Stepover	26	200	200	260	260
WL5B	540 F–B Stepover	27	300	300	420	420
WL5LB	F–B Double Stepover		—	—	500	500
WL7F	720 F–F Stepover		650	650	650	650
WL5F	540 B–F Stepover	28	300	300	420	420
WL5LF	B–F Double Stepover		—	—	500	500
WL7B	720 B–B Stepover		550	550	550	550
TWB	180 F–B Toehold	29	—	—	150	150
TWF	B–F Toehold	30	—	—	150	150
TWO	360 F–F Toehold	31	—	—	300	300
TWBB	B–B Toehold	32	—	—	330	330
TW5B	540 F–B Toehold	33	—	—	500	500
TW5F	B–F Toehold	34	—	—	500	—
TW7F	720 F–F Toehold	35	—	—	650	650
TW7B	B–B Toehold	36	—	—	650	—
TWLB	180 F–B Toehold Stepover	37	—	—	320	—
TWLF	B–F Toehold Stepover	38	—	—	380	—
TWLO	360 F–F Toehold Stepover	39	—	—	480	480
TWLBB	B–B Toehold Stepover	40	—	—	480	480
TWL5B	540 F–B Toehold Stepover	41	—	—	600	600
TWL5F	B–F Toehold Stepover	42	—	—	650	—
WFLIPF	Forward Somersault	43	750	—	750	—
WFLIPB	Backward Somersault	44	700	—	700	—
SLB	180 F–B Ski line	45	—	—	350	350
SLF	B–F Ski line	46	—	—	400	400
SLO	360 F–F Ski line	47	—	—	400	400
SLBB	B–B Ski line	48	—	—	450	450
SL5B	540 F–B Ski line	49	—	—	550	550
SL5F	B–F Ski line	50	—	—	550	550

Trick values

JUMP

With the constant element of danger, jumping is the most exciting and spectacular waterskiing event. And the crowd's favourite. The aim is to carry maximum speed into the ramp, get maximum lift off the ramp and fly the maximum distance from the ramp. Top men will approach the 6 ft (1.8 m) ramp at speeds of 80 m.p.h., so if they make a mistake the falls can be spectacular. The ramp surface is usually fibreglass, waxed and kept wet with running water. The skier is only on the surface a split second, just long enough to straighten his/her legs at the top of the ramp. This so-called 'spring' off the top of the ramp gives the jumper improved trajectory. Today, the top men can soar over 200 ft (61 m), and the top woman, Deena Mapple, can jump nearly 160ft (48.8 m).

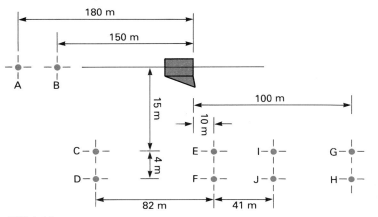

Official jump course

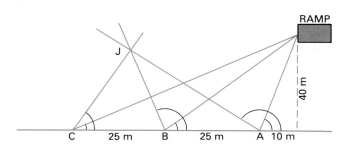

Distance AB = BC = 25 m   A – B – C is a straight line
Jump position relative to A : 10 m back, 40 m out.
Jump is exactly parallel to ABC.

How jump distances are measured

The skiers have three attempts to land the longest jump. In preparing for the jump, they will cut as wide as possible to the side of the boat away from the ramp and then, at the last possible moment, they will make a final cut to the ramp. As they cross the boat's wake, the skier will be experiencing towline forces of three times his/her weight and from that angle the ramp looks like a solid wall, whereas in actual fact it is inclined at an angle of 16 degrees for men and 14 for women. Women and girls use a 1.5 m (5 ft) ramp and boys can use either 1.5 or 1.65 m (5 ft 6 ins) ramp. Men have the choice of using the 1.65 or 1.80 m (6 ft) ramp. Six inches in height may not seem like much, but it makes a huge difference to the angle of the ramp.

The boat is driven down the jump course at a maximum of 57 k.p.h. (35 m.p.h.) for men and 51 k.p.h (32 m.p.h.) for women. Re-runs can occur if the boat is driven at an incorrect speed. The distances are measured from three meter stations, with each station comprising two meters. The average sighting of each meter station is used to measure the distance from the ramp providing the spread between the top and bottom meters is within accepted tolerances. These averages are fed into a computer, which calculates (in official jargon) 'the distance to the centroid of the triangle made by the intersection of the three angles'. In other words, the distance from the ramp to the point where the heels of the skier make their maximum depression in the water (as normally indicated by the spout of water rising after a skier's landing).

6 SLALOM SKIING

BY WORLD CHAMPION, KIM LASKOFF

Kim Laskoff wins her second world title, finishing ahead of Deena Mapple and Susi Graham.

You don't have to be big and strong to kick up a huge wall of spray, carve tight turns or ski round the six buoys in a slalom course. The 1987 and 1989 women's world champion, Kim Laskoff, is only 5 ft 4 ins and weighs just 119 lbs. She reached the top in less than eight years of skiing by using the correct techniques.

Slalom skiing is the ultimate challenge and, ultimately, the course and the boat always beat the skier – although, with good technique, you can win the battle all the way down to the shortest rope lengths. Success in this most exciting and popular form of waterskiing depends on developing good basic skills. These can be learned away from the course while you are free skiing.

The secret to slalom skiing is correct body position. Whether you are an avid recreational skier or a professional who runs 38 off (11.25 m), you must develop and maintain a proper stance – only the correct body position will enable you to resist the pull of the boat. Basically, when you are slalom skiing, you must remember to keep your shoulders back, your hips forward, your knees and ankles bent, and your head up. Sounds easy, doesn't it? However, learning to do all this correctly is one of the most difficult parts of finally mastering the slalom course – I know, it was for me.

When you are practising, you must always strive to maintain this position. When I say 'shoulders back', I mean back and leaning away from the boat. When you are in this position you can resist the boat's pull with your entire body instead of just your arms and back. I always try to arch my back slightly. This pushes my shoulders back and forces my hips forward – two fundamentals of correct body position.

The main difference between the professionals and the amateurs with good style is the amount of 'lean'. If you compare your style with that of the pros pictured in this book, you will probably notice that when you are crossing the wakes and turning, your body is at an angle of 60–80 degrees to the water, the pros are 45 degrees or less. When you can lean properly, you do not have to be extremely strong to run the course on a short line.

You must bend your knees because they are your built-in shock absorbers and will help you to maintain the correct body position when you hit the wakes or rough water. Some skiers bend their knees but then lock them in to that position. Don't do that – keep them flexible. Also, don't squat down – try to push your hips up and forward. Your shoulders, hips and ankles should be in a straight line, even though your body is leaning at an angle away from the boat.

Now that you know the basic stance, let's put it to use in the slalom course. Slalom skiing is a series of cuts and turns. You cut across the wakes, then turn around the buoys. These two acts form the basis of what are generally called the acceleration and deceleration phases. The acceleration phase is obtained by leaning with pull. The

Bend your knees to cut across the wakes.

33

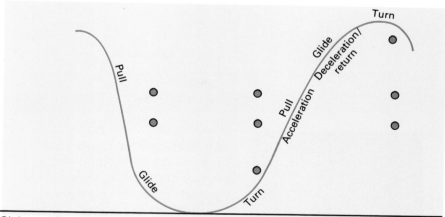

Slalom skiing phases

deceleration phase is a matter of leaning without pull.

Don't look down at the wakes when you are cutting through them. It is a general rule that where your head goes, your body usually follows. So, if you look down, you will probably fall down

34

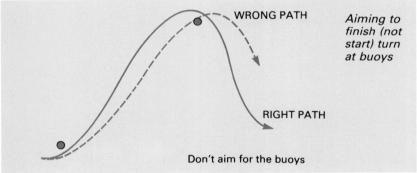

WRONG PATH

Aiming to finish (not start) turn at buoys

RIGHT PATH

Don't aim for the buoys

also. Remember to keep your knees bent and flexible – your knees and the edge of the ski are the best weapons you have as you slice through the wakes. Try to push your knees and ankles forward – this will keep your hips up. When your knees and ankles are bent you have better control of your ski and it cannot be forced off edge and skip out of the water while turning. This is particularly important when you are skiing in rough water. Keep your shoulders back so you can resist the boat's pull. Push your hips forward so they are in front of your shoulders while keeping the handle close to your hip. You must make sure that your shoulders and chest are facing the direction in which you are cutting, so that you can achieve maximum angle. The ideal angle is 90 degrees to the back of the boat.

When you learn how to cut and lean correctly, the buoys on the slalom course will be easier to negotiate. The more angle and lean you get through the wakes, the earlier you will be for the buoys when you start to ski the slalom course. The earlier you are, the more time you will have to decelerate and make a smooth turn round the buoy. You will then be in good form to get a good angle and cut to the next buoy. So, learn the proper lean early on and your transition from free skiing to the slalom course will be that much easier.

As soon as you have completed the lean and cut across the wakes it is time to start the transition to the opposite edge of your ski. This step is commonly known as the *edge change*. During the edge change you are slowing your ski down and preparing to turn. Start decelerating by letting up on your pull as your ski comes off the second wake. Push your knees and ankles forward – this takes the weight off the back of the ski and enables you to change from the accelerating or outside edge to the decelerating or inside edge. Make sure you change edges quickly and that you are never riding on a flat ski. If the ski does go flat, you will gain too much speed into your turn, which will give you slack line and cause you to lose angle. If you find yourself on the flat of the ski, there are a couple of choices for recovery. One is to make a sharp hook turn and try to hang onto the slack line created by this move. Or, you can come slightly down course and make an easier turn and try to make up lost time with an aggressive pull through the wakes. (I prefer this second method and have recovered many times this way.)

During the edge change it is important to maintain the correct body position. You need to have your body in a straight line, head up and shoulders back. Keep your back arched and push your hips, knees and ankles forward. Begin the turn by leaning the way you want to go and take your outside hand off the handle, keeping your free arm in close to your body so that you can grab the handle easily as you complete your turn. Also, if you let your free arm swing around it can cause you to lose your balance. Extend the arm holding the handle to the side towards the boat pylon. Think of the arm as an extension of the

rope, so it should always point to the ski pole as you turn.

Holding the handle with the inside arm and releasing with the outside arm serves two purposes. It extends the length of the line and helps in obtaining lean towards the wake, which helps you decelerate and turn. At this stage, you do not have to extend your arm fully – that is for when you get into shortline slalom skiing.

By the time you have extended your arm, the ski should have slowed down enough to allow you to make a smooth, controlled turn. As you complete the turn, grab the handle with your free hand and start the cut through the wakes again. A common problem skiers have is to reach out in front instead of in line with the ski pole. When they do this they are pulled forward at the waist and the ski loses its edge. When you break at the waist you usually end up falling flat on your face – one of my least favourite falls. While you are learning to cut and turn, I suggest you choose a comfortable speed between 24 and 32 m.p.h. It is important not to go too slowly because your ski will plough through the water and turning will be extremely difficult.

Going too fast can also be very detrimental to good form because too much speed makes it hard for the skier to control the ski. The boat speed you choose will depend on your body weight, size and skill level. Generally, a 100 lb person would start at about 24 m.p.h. whereas a 220 lb skier would need about 32 m.p.h.

When you feel competent at your beginning speed, gradually increase it in increments of 2 m.p.h. At this point it is not necessary to go to the maximum boat speed (36 m.p.h. for men and 34 m.p.h. for women). Stay at the speed at which you feel comfortable so you can work on good basic technique. (Learning good style from the beginning will speed up your progress later on.) I also suggest that you do not use a full 75 ft line, even when you are beginning. Instead, shorten the rope one notch to 15 ft off (18.25 m) and practise at that length. Long line is completely different from all the other rope lengths and often creates extra slack and drag. You may as well begin with a rope length which will help you further 'down the line'.

THE HALF COURSE

Once you are able to cut through the wakes and make aggressive turns consistently, you are ready to tackle the 'mini' or 'half' course. The boat will drive halfway between the boat gates and the right-hand turn buoys (1, 3 and 5). The skier zigzags round the righthand buoys and the boat buoys (first the nearest one and later the outside one). During this stage you learn about timing through the course, become familiar with the layout of the buoys and become comfortable cutting around strange floating objects in the water. I was shocked when I first tried the mini course, I thought I'd make it straight away but, much to my astonishment, it was not as easy as it looked and took me many attempts to master it.

When you begin the mini course, start with the rope at 15 off (18.25 m). You will need to slow the boat to your minimum speed because the buoys are going to come up much quicker than you expect. It is easier to learn the mini course before the full course because the turn buoys are only half as far apart as they are on the full course. Learn the mini course correctly and the transition to the full course will be much easier.

36

The mini course will teach you rhythm and timing – you now have to fit all your pulls, preturn, turn and pulls again into a proper course. Your cuts and turns must remain the same as when you are free skiing, only now they need to be done around buoys at a particular place instead of whenever you feel like it. This will help you keep wide. But, remember, the buoy marks the end of the turn, not the beginning, so aim well to the side of it. If you find you are too late to make it around a buoy, just turn inside it and head for the next one. No matter how many buoys you miss, try to make six consecutive turns because that will help you work on your rhythm.

A common reason for being 'late' to the buoys is not pulling (leaning away from the boat) for long enough. This is my worst problem and I try to think about pulling an extra second or two longer than I feel I should in order to get around the buoy. If you get too much slack line, you may be pulling too long or be too upright, with straight legs, as you turn. The answer is to stop pulling just after the second wake and to keep your knees flexed throughout your turn. Remember to maintain the correct body position at all times.

When you consistently make the half course with correct form, you are ready to try the full course. This is the time when everything I've talked about so far should come together. You must remember what you have learned about body position, rhythm and timing.

THE FULL COURSE

Skiing the full course is a great challenge, whether you are a beginner or a world champion. There is always something further

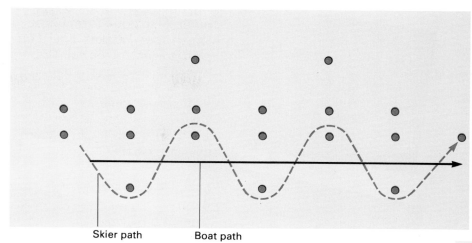

Skier path   Boat path

The mini course

to reach for – another buoy, a higher boat speed, or a shorter rope length, I think this is what makes slalom so exciting for me.

Once again, you will need to stay at 15 off (18.25 m) at a slow boat speed and gradually work up to your maximum speed. As with most things, you cannot learn everything at once. So, during your first attempts at the full slalom course, don't try to go through the entrance gate. Instead, start the course at the number one buoy. Pull wide to the right side of the course at least 10 ft before the entrance gate. Stay on your outside edge, then make a wide, early turn around number one buoy. When you complete the turn, start an aggressive pull through the wakes and head for number two. Remember to maintain the proper body position throughout. As with the half course, when you are too late to make it around the outside of a buoy, turn inside and try for the next one. If you are having trouble getting around buoy number two, start the course there. Cut to the left, then stop your pull and lean right towards

38

Setting up for the entrance gate.

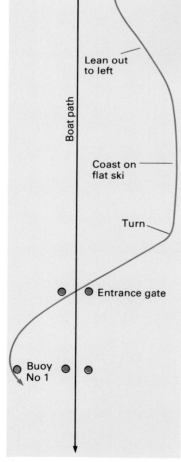

Slalom gate approach

the wake, make an easy turn and then cut to a point well to the right of buoy number three.

When you can run the full course every time in good form, you are ready to try it with the entrance gate.

ENTRANCE GATE

There is no definite formula to tell you exactly when to cut for the gate. Basically, you learn your timing through a process of trial and error. Start by pulling out as wide as you can on the left side of the course. Try to line up with the number two, four and six turn buoys. Once you have pulled out, coast on the flat of the ski and gently push down on the tip so you are able to slow down. Once the ski has slowed sufficiently,

you need to edge and make your cut through the entrance gate and around number one buoy. Deciding when to cut through the gate is the most difficult part. The way I suggest you learn is by picking a part of the boat (bow, ski pole, rear platform, etc.) and when it passes through the gate, make your cut for it.

Slowly rock on to the edge of your ski and cut for number one buoy. If you find that you pass in front of both gate buoys, you are too early and need to pick a point farther back on the boat. If you pass on the inside of the gate buoys, you are too late and need to pick an earlier point on the boat. You should be going through the gate just to the left of the right-hand gate buoy.

With each speed and rope length you will need to make adjustments for the cut through the gate. When you can make the full course with the entrance gate at your maximum speed, you are ready to start shortening the line.

SHORT LINE

A common question asked by skiers is 'What's the difference between 22 off (16 m) and 28 off (14.25 m) and 32 off (13 m)?' Basically, the shorter the rope, the quicker and more aggressive your actions must be. Shortening the rope is equivalent to widening the course.

Twenty-two off feels very similar to 15 ft off. You do not need to lean as far back through the wakes, nor will you need to pull as long to the buoys as you do on the shorter lines. Twenty-eight off will feel a little more difficult. You will need to increase the length of the pulls through the wakes to give yourself more angle for the approach to the next buoy. It is critical that you keep your shoulders back during these shorter rope lengths. At 32 off, you will notice a big difference from the previous rope lengths. Without the correct body position it is virtually impossible to make this pass. Your turns around the buoys need to be sharper and you need to start your pulls out of the turns sooner. It took me 'forever' to finally figure out this pass. Thirty-five and 38 ft off are passes which require precise timing of turns and pulls. You have little room for error, especially at 38 off, because the rope is shorter than the width from the centre of the course to the turn buoy.

WIND

Now that you know how to run the course, you need to learn how to cope with another obstacle – the wind, which makes the slalom course even more difficult.

Now you have to start using your brain as well as your body in the slalom course, and start compensating for the wind which may be a head wind, tail wind or cross wind. A head wind is one which blows directly into your face, while a tail wind blows behind you into your back. Cross winds blow from side to side.

A head wind is preferred by most skiers because it helps them to slow down their ski and keeps slack out of the line. It is important to change your edge closer to the buoy as you turn because you may decelerate too much and ski inside the buoy. The key to head winds is to pull longer than usual through the wake . . . this will help you get wide of the buoy.

A tail wind is often more difficult because it pushes the skier into the buoys. Your ski will often continue to accelerate when you want to slow down for your turn. When you cannot slow down into the turn, the ski will be pulled off edge and you will lose angle. Try to let up early on your pull and push really hard with your knees into the turn. Doing this will help slow down your ski and make it easier to complete your turn.

With a cross wind you have to remember to pull harder into the wind and, when the wind is behind you, you have to increase your lean in the deceleration and turn phase.

ROUGH WATER

In rougher water it is even more important to keep the ski on edge throughout the course.

CONCLUSION

As you learn to ski at the shorter rope lengths it becomes obvious that tall skiers have an advantage, with their extra height and reach. But we short skiers (I'm only 5 ft 4 ins) are still able to run good slalom by using correct techniques. Correct slalom style can compensate for lack of height and reach, and allow the less muscular, shorter skiers to compete with the taller, stronger ones.

Each step along the way takes a good deal of concentration and hard work. Don't be discouraged when certain steps are more difficult to learn than others. I still have a million things I need to improve upon. This constant challenge is what makes slaloming so much fun. Sometimes you have to regress to perfect a new step along the way. Don't be too proud to go back a step. If you are having problems at a particular rope length, try it at a slower speed and build from there. Just be patient and you will find all the hard work will pay off as you master the slalom course.

TRICK SKIING

7

BY WORLD AND OLYMPIC CHAMPION, RICKY McCORMICK MBE

Ricky McCormick is one of the greatest waterskiers of all time. Although he became an excellent three-eventer, he made his greatest impact in tricks. 'Tricky Ricky', as he came to be called, is credited with developing and adding more than six tricks to the rule book, including 540-degree turns (front to back and back to front), stepover 360s (front to back and back to front), stepover 540s (front to back and back to front), and the wake gainer flip.

His love of air and enthusiasm for tricks led him to a string of eight consecutive trick victories at the US Nationals from 1964 onwards. But he also won eight National overall crowns as well, including three in a row in Open Men beginning in 1977. He represented the US at the World Championships six times, from 1967 to 1979, winning gold medals in tricks in 1971 and in jumping two years later.

In 1972 he joined two other US skiers in West Germany, when waterskiing was made a demonstration sport at the Munich Olympics. He dazzled the crowds and won gold medals in tricks and jumping.

42

Other career highlights include being the first male skier to win back-to-back US Masters overall titles in 1970 and 1971, then following it up with two more tremendous overall victories in 1975 and 1977. He retired from competition in 1982 and was recently elected to the Water Ski Hall of Fame in the Water Ski Museum and Hall of Fame in Winter Haven, Florida. Now he is helping Sea Ray develop a tournament ski boat.

I have been trick skiing almost as long as I can remember, since I was about five, and as I look back there are a few basics that stand out in my mind as the most important tips in learning to be a good tricker:

1 Learn to set your bindings a little tighter than normal for good ankle control.

2 Always hold the handle with your palms down, not one hand on top and one on the bottom.

3 Be able to cut on your trick skis and jump wakes. This will help your balance, for the trick skis have no rudders but do have grooves.

4 Legs should be bent a little before tricks, straighter in the trick and bent more at the finish. The lower your centre of gravity, the easier the trick.

5 For turn-around tricks, the handle comes into the body with a steady pull, not putting slack in the rope. Pull the handle to the opposite hip you are turning, making it easier and faster to grasp the handle backwards. (When backwards, your palms will be facing up.)

6 If you are pulled over toward the boat while skiing backwards, lower the handle below your backside, where it will have less leverage on your body. Same goes if you turn backwards and you fall away from the boat – pass the handle higher in the back area.

7 Skis should be no wider than shoulder-width apart, preferably closer. This will give you more surface area to turn on. One thing that will tell you when they are too wide is if when you are turning you keep losing one ski.

8 When you are riding your skis, think of controlling them, but don't turn so hard that you over control them.

9 Practise every trick on dry land first. I do a good deal of dry-land practising to perfect the positioning of the rope. To me, trick skiing is all about rope handling. The axis point of the body that I use is the hips. I try to keep the handle located right at my hips, so that when I pull in the handle is easy to pass from one hand to the other.

10 The trick skier should try to push his hips or twist into the tricks and this can be practised on dry land as easily as on the water. You can figure where the handle should be, the correct body position, where to put your head and your shoulders before you go on the water where you might waste valuable time falling.

11 Try to use a 14-inch handle, so when you do a turn the handle will be almost the width of your body and you won't have to reach so far around your back.

12 Boat speed for best tricking depends mostly on the size of the skier. If you weigh 180–190 lbs, try a speed of 18–20 m.p.h. The lighter you are, the slower the speed. Your rope length, which should be about 35–45 ft, can be set by doing a side slide. Put the tips of your skis to the place

where the wake starts up – the wake should be about two feet. You should try to be right at the peak of the converging wake, yet not so far into the rooster tail that your skis are catching in the turbulence. Before we look at the techniques involved in doing individual tricks, here are a few pointers that I think might help the beginner:

Your *knees* guide you into all tricks. When you want to make a turn to the right, you swing your flexed knees to the right. If you keep your knees too straight, you will have to move your whole body into the turn. In trick skiing, you want to keep your back and waist straight and let your knees (and sometimes your head) do the leading. A word of caution: don't put too much head into a turn because you will have a tendency to over control what you are doing and get lost in your spin.

To me, trick skiing is the most fun of all the events. That is what it should be for you. Sure, it takes work, but the work should be fun and as long as it is fun to learn the trick, the excitement comes from making the first one. That is part of the fun of tricking. So start right and I'll be seeing you with a winner's trophy before you know it!

Here are some of the building block tricks. It might take you two years to learn them, but you need to learn them well before you can progress to the more difficult and spectacular tricks, like the wake flip. As soon as you have learned a trick, then learn its reverse, which will also score points. For example, if you've learned a turn turning to the left, now learn it turning to the right. The technique is the same.

Correct basic stance: Knees and ankles bent to centre weight over your skis with the majority of weight on the balls of your feet, skis about 10 cm apart, back straight, overhand grip keeping the handle at waist level, head up and shoulders level.

Correct basic backward position: knees and ankles bent, majority of weight on balls of your feet, handle held with palms up, close to the small of your back, head and shoulders up. Look at the horizon – not down.

BASIC SURFACE TRICK

Side slide
(One and two skis)
METHOD

1 Establish correct trick stance and body position.

2 Rotate flexed knees to desired direction away from boat.

3 Pull handle down at waist level to hip closest to the boat.

4 Release hand farthest from the boat to the side for balance.

5 To return to front position, re-grasp handle with free hand and rotate back to the front position.

44

BASIC SURFACE TRICK

180° front to back
METHOD

1 Establish correct trick stance and body position.

2 Pull handle down and to the desired hip while rotating knees in the direction of your turn. Keep head up and shoulders level.

3 Keep pulling on handle, keeping it close to your body so it is easy to grasp when you reach the back position.

4 Hands should grasp handle to the small of your back.

5 Keep head up and work on your stance in the back position.

6 Your knuckles should be against your back.

BASIC SURFACE TURN

180° back to front
METHOD

1 While you have your back to the boat, establish the correct body position and stance.

2 Release with one hand from the handle while pulling the handle in with the opposite hand.

3 Keep the handle close to your body.

4 Feel for the pull of the rope and follow the pull to the front position. Use your knees and head to turn.

BASIC WAKE TRICK

180° wake front to back
METHOD

1 Establish correct trick stance and body position.

2 You should be directly behind the boat between the wakes.

3 Beginning the trick, push knees forward as you edge toward the wake.

4 As you get close to the wake begin to pull the handle toward your body and hip enough to start the rotation.

5 Your body should be upright and shoulders level.

6 At the crest of the wake, lead turn with head and shoulders. Keep a vertical axis and release hand from handle for desired direction.

7 Reach for the handle with free hand behind back.

8 Use knees to absorb impact of landing.

9 Upon landing, body should still have vertical stance.

BASIC WAKE TRICK

180° wake back to front
METHOD

1 Skiing backwards, establish correct body position and stance.

2 You should be no more than 3 ft outside the wake.

3 Turn skis and edge towards the wake.

4 Release hand closest to the wake at the crest of the wake.

5 Lead with head and shoulders toward the front position, regrasping handle with free hand.

6 Flex knees on landing to absorb the 'shock'.

BASIC WAKE TRICK

360° wake front to front
METHOD

1 Establish correct body position and stance.

2 You should be about 3 ft outside the wake. The arm closest to the wake will be holding the handle behind your back with your knuckles on lower back; the other hand will be holding rope in front of you.

3 Push knees forward and edge toward the wake.

4 At the crest of the wake, release hand on rope and lead spin by turning your head in the direction you want to go.

5 Keep your head up and shoulders level to maintain a good vertical axis.

6 Keep handle in close to your body, so when you get forward from the spin you can grasp the handle quickly with the free hand.

7 Bend knees to absorb shock of landing.

BASIC STEPOVER TRICK

Back to front stepover
Note: It is probably easier to learn the back to front turn before the front to back because it is always easier to return to a familiar position.
METHOD

1 Establish correct body position and stance backward.

2 Reach between legs and grasp handle with the right hand if you are stepping over the rope with your right leg, with your left hand if you are stepping over the rope with your left leg.

3 Place free hand to the side for balance.

4 Start lifting ski to step over the line, bending your leg slightly.

5 Rotate your head and shoulders toward the front position and your body will follow.

6 As you come to the front position, grasp handle with your free hand.

BASIC WAKE STEPOVER TRICK

180° front to back
METHOD

1 Establish correct body position and stance.

2 You should be between both wakes behind boat.

3 Gradually pull rope in with arms straight. Turn head and shoulder toward back position.

4 With low handle position, lift ski (or free foot) over the rope and at the same time turn 180° toward the back position.

5 Bend leg as it passes over line.

6 Release free hand for balance.

7 Establish correct stance with head up.

BASIC WAKE STEPOVER TRICK

180° step front to back
METHOD

1 Establish correct body position and stance.

2 Be behind boat in centre of wakes.

3 Edge toward wakes while pulling with arm straight down and in towards waist.

4 Shift body weight to ski you are not stepping with.

5 Swing your ski or foot up to the towline.

6 Release free hand for balance.

7 Lead with head and shoulders toward back position.

8 Ski should follow in 180° turn.

9 Keep head up and lean slightly away from boat.

47

BASIC WAKE STEPOVER

180° back to front

METHOD

1 Ride in back stepover position about 3 ft from wake.

2 Use free hand for balance.

3 Keep head up.

4 Edge toward wake.

5 Shift weight to ski that is staying in the water and pick up the opposite leg.

6 Lift ski leg or foot over the line keeping leg bent while it passes over the rope.

7 As the turn begins, reach with free hand toward handle and grasp it.

8 When landing in front position, bend knees to absorb shock.

TOEHOLDS (BASIC STANCE)

Head up, shoulders square, back straight, legs bent. Make sure the foot in the toe piece fits securely. To get your foot into the toehold bridle, slowly bring your free foot up to the toe piece, but keep this leg bent as you do so. At the same time, bring the rope down to meet your foot halfway. Concentrate on maintaining balance and staying upright over the ski. Once you have let go of the handle, be prepared to resist the pull.

BASIC TOEHOLD TRICK

180° front to back surface

METHOD

1 Establish correct body position and stance with foot in strap.

2 Bend both knees.

3 Both arms are used for balance.

4 By using your ski leg, twist knee and ski toward back position keeping weight over binder.

5 Keep body erect and head up.

6 Make sure slow movements for turns are very easy.

BASIC TOEHOLD TRICK

Toe back to front
METHOD

1 Establish correct body position and stance with foot in toe strap.

2 Arms out for balance.

3 Head up and body erect.

4 Pull toe leg in slightly to relieve pressure on rope.

5 Turn head and shoulders toward front position.

6 Keep weight over binder and reach toward handle to keep weight forward.

BASIC TOE WAKE TRICK

Toehold wake front to back and back to front
METHOD
Use the same procedures as we used for the surface turns, keeping in mind two things:

1 Edge toward wake, don't cut hard.

2 Pull harder with toe leg in strap when turning.

EQUIPMENT

Trick skiing requires a special pair of short, wide skis. They are stiff, slippery and have no fin (so you can turn right round). When you get the feel for these skis, you can drop one and perform the tricks on just one ski.

Boat – does not have to be as powerful as those used for slalom and jumping. Usual speed range is 12–22 m.p.h.

Trick release – important for toe tricks. Must be operated by an experienced coach or trick skier.

Rope and handle – 14-inch handle is best, attached to a rope of 35–45 ft.

Trick skies are short, wide, stiff and slippery.

Here is a sample of a trick run,
using tricks from this chapter.

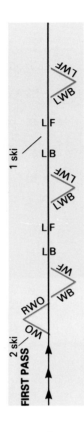

50

FIRST PASS			
Skis	Tricks	Code	Points
2	Wake 360° front to front	WO	110
2	Reverse	RWO	110
2	Wake 180° front to back	WB	50
2	Wake 180° back to front	WF	50
2	Step over 180° front to back	LB	70
2	Step over 180° back to front	LF	70
2	Wake step 180° front to back	LWB	110
2	Wake step 180° back to front	LWF	110
1	Step over 180° front to back	LB	110
1	Step over 180° back to front	LF	110
1	Wake step 180° front to back	LWB	160
1	Wake step 180° back to front	LWF	160
		Total	1220

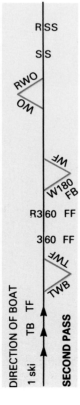

SECOND PASS			
Skis	Tricks	Code	Points
1	Toe hold 180° front to back	TB	100
1	Toe hold 180° back to front	TF	100
1	Wake toe hold front to back	TWB	150
1	Wake toe hold back to front	TWF	150
1	Water surface turn 360°	360FF	90
1	Reverse	R360FF	90
1	Wake 180° front to back	W180FB	80
1	Wake 180° back to front	WF	80
1	Wake 360°	WO	150
1	Reverse	RWO	150
1	Side slide	SS	40
1	Reverse	RSS	40
			1220
		Add first pass	1220
			2440

MORE ADVANCED TRICKS

Wake 540° front to back
METHOD

1 Establish vertical body position and stance.

2 You should wrap the same as the wake 360°. Arm closest to the wake will be behind the back with knuckles on the lower back. Be outside the wake about 3 ft.

3 Push knees forward and edge toward the wake. Keep shoulders square to the boat.

4 At the crest of the wake, release hand on the rope and lead with the head toward the direction of the spin.

5 Holding head up and shoulders level will help keep a good axis.

6 Keep handle close to body for a quicker spin. As you come forward, grasp the handle with the free hand, still turning the head to the back position.

7 You will land with both hands on the handle (think of spinning fast rather than jumping).

Wake 540° back to front
METHOD

1 Establish back vertical stance.

2 Be outside the wake about 3 ft. Both hands on handle, head and upper body mostly turned toward the boat.

3 Begin to edge toward the wake with stance over feet and ski. Begin to pull with arm farthest from boat.

4 At the crest of the wake, give a quick hard pull with the far arm and lead with the head toward the direction of the spin.

5 Keep handle in close to the body. As you move forward, grasp the handle quickly with the free hand.

6 Bend knees to absorb the landing.

Stepover 360° front to front
METHOD

1 Skier should be outside wake about 3 ft. If right foot forward, on the right-hand side.

2 To wrap for trick will be like wake 360° front to front. Left hand will be behind knee or just little higher, knuckles to the back side of the knee.

3 Keep weight on the front ball of the foot while edging to wake. Shoulders should be in front of the front foot.

4 Release the rope with the right hand and turn the head toward the spin.

5 At the moment you start the turn, bend up the free leg to the body.

6 When landing, the right hand needs to grasp the handle before you land on the water.

7 Give with the leg you ski on, on the landing.

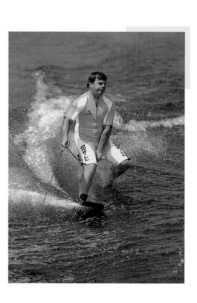

Stepover 360° back to back
METHOD

1 Skier should be outside wake about 3 ft.

2 Assume the line back position with foot touching the water.

3 With the vertical body position, begin to edge to the wake.

4 In sequence at the crest of the wake: draw the free leg up toward the body, begin to pull on the handle to keep close to the body and turn the head toward the spin.

5 The handle must be kept close in throughout the whole trick so on the landing it can be given into the boat to recover from the trick while turning forward.

6 The free leg needs to be kept in close to the body for balance.

7 You may land with one hand on the handle. Giving with the ski leg by lowering the body centre of gravity will increase your success rate.

Ski line back
METHOD

1 If right foot forward, ski should be on right-hand side outside the wake about 3 ft.

2 Get in good solid vertical stance, with arms out, while edging to the wake.

3 At the crest of the wake, body should be advanced to the handle without slack rope.

4 The handle comes in and down to the left side, with the legs drawing up to the body.

5 To turn backwards, rotate the handle and the wrist until your little finger is on the top.

6 After the ski passes over the rope, straighten your legs back out in mid air.

7 This trick may be landed with one or both hands.

Wake gainer or back flip
METHOD

1 If right foot forward, skier should be outside the left-hand wake about 3 ft (no more than 4 ft).

2 Stand down on both feet in the vertical stance and edge relatively hard to the wake.

3 Hands will be out away from the body and legs slightly bent.

4 At the crest, the sequence is: legs straighten, handle comes in and the head goes back, leading the turn.

5 The tighter the rope is kept to the body, the faster the spin will be.

6 One or two hands may be used for the landing.

7 The landing may take a few times to ski away.

Toe wake 360° front to front
METHOD

1 If right foot forward, be outside right-hand wake with left foot behind right knee and strap on left foot.

2 Be outside wake about 2 ft, weight on the ball of the foot, right hand on rope, left hand free for balance.

3 Keep weight forward and edge toward the wake.

4 At the crest of the wake, release the hand on the rope and lead with the head toward the direction of the spin.

5 Keep shoulders level for a good axis.

6 Keep toe handle foot close to the back of the knee through the spin to keep from falling over away from the boat.

7 Bend slightly forward at the waist, as if grasping the handle, to keep body position forward for the landing.

Ricky halfway through a back flip and (bottom) *setting up for a toe wake 360.*

52

JUMPING

8

BY WORLD CHAMPION, MIKE HAZELWOOD MBE

'Two hundred feet jumps are usually pretty easy,' says Mike Hazelwood MBE. 'That's funny to say, but they are easy if you turn in the right spot, cut all the way to the jump, and get your good, nice pull, kick straight up and then you get this huge pull from the boat because you want to go straight up and the boat wants to pull you straight forward. You know when it's a great jump – it feels right and you get that float at the end. It feels real easy – no stress on your body or anything. It's when you're fighting it that it's hard.'

Throughout his illustrious career, Mike Hazelwood has constantly pushed the limits of how far a man can jump. In 1980, at the Moomba Masters, he extended the world record by an incredible 2.4 m (7.9 ft). A year later he pushed the boundaries even further by jumping 60 m, and then in 1986, at the Iron Man Championships in Alabama, USA, he set a new world record of 61.9 m (203 ft). Although Mike, who retired from competitive skiing in 1989, will be remembered for his huge leaps, he has also won numerous tricks and slalom titles and in 1977, at the age of 19, was crowned overall world champion. In 1979 and 1981, he also won the world jump titles. At the 1983 Worlds, he won the silver in overall.

His list of major triumphs began when he was 15 and took the British slalom title. A year later, in 1974, he became the British overall and tricks champion. In the years that followed he won most of the world's major titles, including seven victories in the US Masters, became the first European to win the Australian Moomba Masters overall title and in 1983, 1986 and 1987 he was crowned the Coors Light Water Ski Tour jump champion. In 1987, he was the leading male money winner on the United States pro tour, helped by some magnificent and consistent jumping.

Jumping is the most exciting, the most spectacular . . . and the most dangerous discipline in waterskiing. But there are few thrills which can compare to that of flying through the air on a pair of skis. In fact, waterski jumpers travel further over the flat surface of the earth than any other sportsmen, including stunt motorcyclists like Evil Knevil. And the amazing thing is, you don't have to jump that far to experience this thrill – just going over the ramp and landing will do it.

Of course, once you have done that you will want to go on – soaring 50 feet, then aiming for 80, then 100, then 120, then 150, then 180, then 200, then the world record. Jumping is not that difficult to learn. If you get the basics right, it is very easy to jump 100 feet. And think, if you were doing that 40 years ago, you would have been world champion.

Learning to jump is always an exciting prospect, but you should treat the ramp with respect. While you are learning the basics it should be set at the lowest height, which is 5 ft (1.5 m) high, and the boat speed should be between 22 and 28 m.p.h., depending on the skier's weight. A rough weight/speed guide would be:

100 lbs, 22 m.p.h.; 160 lbs, 25 m.p.h.; 200 lbs, 28 m.p.h.

This is all on approximately 70-inch long jump skis.

I recommend that a first-time jumper either goes to a ski school or has a fully qualified instructor in the boat, to coach the skier. Jumping is not difficult when you have an experienced coach in the boat, but can be dangerous without. The more experience the coach has, or the better reputation he has, the safer you are going to be and the easier it is going to be to learn. Jumping is not necessarily dangerous as long as you know what you are doing and you are being guided by a coach who knows what he is doing, e.g. can set the correct ramp height, drive the boat at the right speed and so forth.

The first thing a skier should do on the road to becoming a jumper is to go out and ride his jump skis – crossing the wake, jumping the wake and generally getting accustomed to the skis. The chances are that you have not been on a pair of skis since you learned to drop a ski, so you must get used to skiing on two skis again. Spend 15–20 minutes riding them around.

When you feel comfortable on the skis, then you can start thinking about jumping. The basic skiing position is: skis shoulder width apart, knees bent forward with weight on toes, body bent slightly at waist so your shoulders are just in front of your knees (but don't stick your backside out), arms into waist, handle held with left palm up and right palm down, head up and equal weight on both skis.

Now, ski around in this position. Make sure your knees are pushed forward on the skis, your shoulders are up and your arms are in. Cut around, jump the wakes, land and generally get the feel of jumping. The higher you can get off the wakes and the more aggressive you are, the better you will feel when you go over the jump.

To get the feel of the ramp, ski across the bottom right corner. The boat will have to be driven at an angle of 45 degrees to the ramp. The driver should aim for the 15 and 19 m guide buoys. Let the boat pull you across the bottom right corner of the jump (see diagram A p. 56). The boat will naturally pull you towards the centre of the wakes. Let it. Keep equal weight on both feet and just freeze. The jump is fast, rather like hitting ice.

Anybody who has skied knows that if you ride a little wide of the boat, the boat is going to pull you back towards the wakes. That's all right; that's the line you want to take when you go over the jump first time. Ski outside the left-hand

One of Mike's students, Marc Grinhaff, shows how beginners should work their way up the ramp to get a feel for it.

56

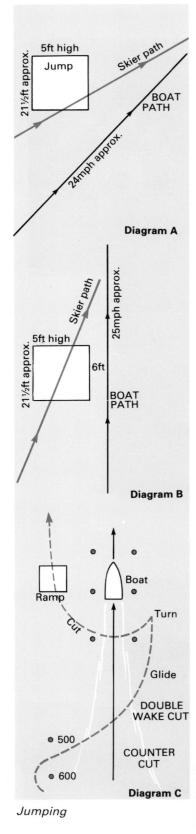

Jumping

wake, look at the ramp and just follow a line straight to the driver. When you are about 25 ft from the ramp, make sure your weight is evenly distributed over both skis and that neither ski is on edge. Think of it like this: you are going to be aiming for the boat and cruising toward the centre of the wakes and the jump is just going to be an obstacle in your path.

So, pull out to the left side, then go over the jump about a foot up. This is going to give you a feel of the jump, let you see how slippery it is and give you an idea of what it is like hitting a solid object at that speed. Remember to stay on your toes – the waxed and watered ramp surface is twice as fast as water.

Once you have made it over the jump safely you can go a little bit higher. Keep your arms down, pushing the handle down to your thighs. This will help keep your shoulders forward and the weight over your skis. Many learners fall

Correct form on the ramp and coming over the top.

because they bring the handle above the waist. Aim towards the boat and skip across the ramp, probably two feet up from the bottom right corner. Once you are comfortable doing this, start going higher up the ramp and straightening out the boat path until you are skiing from the bottom left corner of the ramp to the top right-hand corner.

Once you have made that, you can think about going over the top. Aim for the bottom left corner, put the boat just outside the jump around 26 m.p.h. (42 k.p.h) and ride straight over the jump from bottom left to top right. Let the boat drag you over the jump. The main thing to master when jumping is riding over the jump. This may sound stupid, but riding over the surface and coming off straight is the hard part. Once in the air and straight, learning to land is no problem. As in diagram B, line up just left of the middle, bend your knees, keep your arms in, head up, have equal weight on both feet and your skis approximately 12 inches apart. Set up about 40 feet before the jump, letting the boat tow you on its natural line up and over the jump. Stay still in the air. When landing, try to land just as you would jumping off a chair: knees forward, tips up, with weight just about centre of the balls of the feet. Keep your arms in and YOU'VE MADE IT, YOU'RE A JUMPER!

The key to riding safely over the ramp is body position. Keep your arms down, your weight on your toes, and equal weight on both feet. Your feet should be about a foot apart, with your weight centred over your skis. Then, just let the boat pull you straight over the top. When you land, bend your knees. Try to land on your feet with your arms in, head up and looking straight ahead.

Don't worry about getting air until you make it over the top most of the time. The hardest part is getting over the jump in a good body position, going through the air is no problem because you are still over your feet. Once you have made that, then it is time to start working on distance and the single wake cut. It is stupid to start cutting at a slower speed because what you are trying to do is build speed, so put the speed of the boat up and move the boat out to give you more distance and more control. When you feel comfortable at, say, 28 m.p.h., move up to 30, and once you feel comfortable with the boat in between the jump and 15 m buoy, move it out wider each time. Don't rush it, just do it a bit at a time so you always feel comfortable with what you are doing.

So now the boat should be going about 5 ft to the left of the inside (15 m) guide buoy, and in a straight line parallel to the ramp. The speed should be put up from 28 to 30 m.p.h. Putting the boat out wider and increasing the speed means you are going to get more pull from the boat and will fly further, but it is going to keep the line tighter so you will have more control. You can practise cutting without using a ramp. When you cut, always put more weight on your right ski than your left. Do this by exerting downward pressure on the inside of your right knee. The harder you cut the more weight you will have to transfer to your right foot. On an easy cut you should have about 60 per cent of your weight on your right foot and 40 on your left. On some of my longest jumps I have had, say, 90–95 per cent of my weight on my right foot and I have seen some skiers with the actual left ski in the air. This is not a bad thing because when you are cutting at a very advanced stage,

you want to aim to have 100 per cent of your weight on your right leg.

As well as transferring weight to your right foot when you are cutting, you should also turn your left shoulder away from the pull of the boat. This will drop the left edge of the right ski further in the water and help you push away from the boat. Practise cutting until the position becomes second nature, then set yourself up just outside the left-hand wake and cut for the ramp. To start with, just try edging gently all the way to the jump and ride straight up the middle of the jump. Instead of heading towards the boat, you are going to start heading away from the boat. This angle creates more distance. While you are at this basic stage, take it easy and edge all the way to the jump, pulling with your left arm. To get your spring (lift) off the ramp, try to push your left arm down, your right hand down and bring your hips towards the handle. That will give you your lift. It is no good coming towards the jump with your shoulders down and just trying to throw your shoulders up in the air. That is not the way to spring. Your spring wants to work with your cut, and the best way to do that is to edge all the way to the jump and bring your hips to the handle.

So when you are cutting to the jump now you are going to start going from the boat wakes. Just inside the boat wakes, start and give a gentle edge all the way to the centre of the jump. You should always aim for the centre because it gives you a margin for error. From the centre of the ramp you should travel up to – and take off from – the top left-hand corner. I recommend looking at the middle or, if it feels more comfortable, the top left. Many jumpers look at the top left and have success with it. Looking at the top left corner, or even right over the top of the jump, will help you keep your head and shoulders up. If you find it difficult, or it throws you off balance, try looking at the centre or the middle left. I prefer to look at the centre of the jump. Neither way is right or wrong – it depends which works for you. But don't look at the bottom right-hand corner as you approach the ramp. If you do that, your shoulders will be down, your head is going to be down, and you are going to start hitting the corner, which can be dangerous.

Once you feel comfortable with a cut, start leaving it a little later. Always concentrate on good technique. Keep the boat speed at 30 m.p.h., just outside the 15 m buoy. Dauphins and juniors may prefer to go a little slower – about 28 m.p.h. Heavier skiers can go up to 32 m.p.h. at this stage but, generally, I would recommend 30 as the best speed.

Now you can go just outside the wakes. Same thing again – turn easy, get your right ski around, left shoulder back, arms in, and cut all the way to the jump. The idea is always cut towards the centre of the jump – keep cutting, don't turn back. The power of your cut should be progressive, so you are pulling your hardest just before you hit the ramp. If you start too hard on your cut, then you might be early and have to turn back towards the boat (flatten off). This creates slack, and you will lose power and control. Once you have a tight line, and you have direction away from the boat, you are going to have control. Once you turn back, you have no control. The line is your control when you are jumping – it can save you. If you are in trouble as you leave the ramp, don't let go of that handle – and keep a tight line. You always want a tight line because if you are too far back, you can pull in on the handle, and that is going to bring you over your skis. If you drop your skis behind you, you can use the handle as a pivot point and bring your skis back under you. Follow through on your jump. You don't want to hit the jump and think everything is done. Work on your spring and remember to bring your hips to the handle.

Three-quarter cutting is all about learning good technique: a good edge into the jump, keeping your direction away from the boat, bringing your hips to the handle and getting lift. The theory is that if you go wider, turn smoothly and edge all the way into the jump using this technique, you will be going so fast it will be a 180 ft jump if you do it properly. Starting from just outside the wakes, you can build as much speed as you, at your level, can handle and still get your lift. Gradually you can go out wider and wider.

So you are at 30 or 32 m.p.h., you are on a 5 ft jump and you are edging all the way into the jump – and getting good lift off it. It is time to move out wider. Now what you do is go out wider of the boat until you are nearly 60

degrees to it. Start your turn easy and use the techniques you have already learned. You are going to have a longer distance to travel, therefore you are going to get more speed and more pull off the jump, and it is now going to be important to keep your shoulders up. You probably had your shoulders down a little before but you must now keep your shoulders right up to stop you rotating over the front of your skis. Keep your shoulders up, but your knees forward, and your weight more on the toes of your feet. Cut all the way through the jump. Make sure you don't drop your shoulders, like some students I have seen. They want to 'drop the shoulder' – that is, put the left shoulder towards the water. Don't drop your shoulder down to the water – twist it away from the boat. When you make your turn, put your right ski in front of you and twist your whole body away from the boat. That way you are going to be able to keep your direction. So, you make your turn and keep heading in that direction, pulling harder as you get closer to the jump. When you hit the ramp, bring your hips

towards the handle and pull. In the air, you want to be moving out over your skis. Push your chest forward, but keep your tips up. Pull in on the handle until you hit your peak, then just float down to the water. The best landing is a straight leg landing. Just push your chest over the skis, keep your tips up, and come down as if you were jumping off a chair.

Once you have mastered that landing, you will realise it is the safest way to land. You are not always going to be able to make that landing because you are not always going to be in a good enough position, but once you have mastered that technique it will clean up your landings generally and make your jumping more solid. If you don't have that good a landing at your disposal, then you are always going to be worried on your long distance jumps. Some jumpers have a reputation for not riding out their jumps, and it can play on your mind if you don't think you can make your long jumps. One day you are going to have that beautiful long jump and then going to lose it because you cannot make the landing. So, always work on cleaning up your landings. Don't settle for a sloppy landing – make it clean.

Once you are making your three-quarter cuts and you have gradually built your speed up to the maximum (35 m.p.h. for men and 32 m.p.h. for women), you can start asking for a split. The boat driver will then run straight between the 15 and 19 m buoys. I figure the split or a 'narrow split' is best because you can get a good edge into the ramp and a good pull. That is where I used to jump myself. On some sites, if the water was slow or the driver was driving a little wider than usual, I would ask for a 'narrow split'.

By going to a wider cut, and moving the boat out to a split (between the 15 m and 19 m buoys), you are going to have more room to dig in towards the ramp. Run your split just outside the wakes and keep your skis down through the wakes. You don't want to get air through these wakes, you want to push your foot forward and pull hard just before them. Make sure your skis are on edge and that you are driving right through the wakes. If your ski is flat, then you are going to be getting air and turned around towards the boat. Get your ski on edge and cut all the way to the ramp, making sure you slice right through those wakes. Don't let your left shoulder get turned towards the boat – keep digging in towards the ramp. When you make your turn, you don't need to look at the jump: look away from the jump and cut. Then, as you come towards the wake, pick up the jump and look at the middle or top left of the jump.

When you have mastered this stage, you can start working with the 600 and 500 ft buoys. These buoys are markers to help you on your counter cut. Your counter cut is the cut to set you up for your cut to the jump. What you want to do is to cut *before* the 600. Just before the 600, make your turn and be aggressive. The idea is to get wide, so you make your hard turn on the 600. Do a slalom turn, get your right arm out, curl the turn on your left ski, crank the skis around, then pull as hard as you can to the first wake. Push off the first wake and land on your left ski. I have found this way to be the best because two skis are quite difficult to control through the wakes. Land on your left ski, lift your right ski up and give a good solid dig as hard as you can out to

the right of the boat. Pull all the way to around 45 degrees angle to the boat, then flatten off. Get on the front of the ski and let the ski ride. Then, accelerate past the boat. (You will do this automatically if you have dug in hard enough and have twisted your shoulders away from the boat on your counter cut.) After achieving a successful wide cut, it is important to make a good turn. As you extend your left arm you should begin to bend the left knee in preparation for the weight transfer onto the right ski. Shifting your weight on to the right leg, bend the left ski over and turn your right ski as far to the left as possible. As you rotate the ski, bring the left hand across with a straight arm and grasp the handle with the right hand on the right hip. Begin your push slowly and increase the power as you travel through the cut. If you find you are arriving at the ramp too early, slow down the start of your cut and build the power progressively, or move the boat path out two feet.

To recap: make a smooth turn; wait for the pull of the boat; then make sure you are on your right ski, your left shoulder is back, and your shoulders are up. Make your turn and head straight for the centre of that jump, building angle all the way into it and cutting all the way to the centre. Then, make sure you have got your arms down and your shoulders are up when you are on the ramp. Bring your hips towards the handle, keep going straight ahead through the air, push your chest out and, as you are coming down, spot the landing. Don't look down – look straight ahead and get a feel for when you are going to touch down. Land and ski away. A tip for you if the water is mirror calm: before you jump, make sure you go past the landing area. This will break up the water so you don't get the mirror effect: as you are coming down, you have no idea where to land because all you can see is your reflection in the calm water. I had this happen one time and prelanded. Other problems are head and tail winds. If there is a tail wind, cut out further earlier. Go out about 20 ft before the 600 buoy, depending on which skis you are on and your level, and cut straight out wide. If there is a head wind, cut later.

TRIPLE CUTTING

What the top skiers do to get out wide on the 600 buoy is to make a triple cut. That is, their first cut is from right to left, the same as they will be using towards the jump. To set yourself up for this, swing out just a little to the right of the boat and time your cut so you cut all the way to the left on the 600, so you are wide of the 600. Make a hard turn on the 600, slice through the wakes, push on the first wake, land on your left ski, twist your shoulders away from the boat, and pull as hard as you can at 45 degrees. That will keep your acceleration going. Go on to a flat ski and ride on the front of the ski with your shoulders up. That way you will keep going past the boat. If your ski is on an edge, it is going to slow down and you will not get wide of the boat. In fact, you want to catch up the boat and accelerate past it, as well as getting as wide as you can. You want to be wide when you start your cut because you will have more time and distance to create speed. Also, it is easier to get angle in the turn if you have gone past the boat. In a head wind, it is more difficult to get wide; in a tail wind, it's a piece of cake. So, it might be better to practise this, in the beginning, on a tail wind day. Make an easy turn, let the ski roll around your body as if your left shoulders are the pivot point. When the pull of the boat comes, pull progressively harder all the way to the centre of the jump. If you want to avoid the hole that skiers sometimes drop into, and which slows down the start of their cut, start your turn earlier and make a longer turn on your right ski. That will keep you higher on the water and get you accelerating to the ramp smoother than if you get in a hole – a stop-and-go technique. When you make your turn, pull your handle with your left arm to your right hip. This will stop your backside from sticking out. Keep your head up. Make your turn and bring your left arm to your right hip, pushing your right knee forward, bending both knees in the turn. Get angle from the start of your turn. Keep your shoulders up, knees forward, and keep accelerating all the way to the jump, maintaining your angle away from the boat. You want to go across the jump – don't turn towards the boat. Keep your shoulders square of the top of the jump, and, through the air, pull your arms in and float down. Flex your knees on landing and ride it out – you now have the knowledge to jump 200 ft-plus.

EQUIPMENT

Jump skis – have to be tough and light, so they are made of the latest space-age materials, like Kevlar and graphite fibres. That's why they can cost over £2,000 a pair. The skier's feet are attached by safety bindings made of rubber.

Helmet – made of tough, light plastic. Some have face guards.

Jump suit – wetsuits with built-in flotation. Some have built-in knee braces.

Arm sling – looks like a seat belt attached around the waist. This device helps keep your arms close to your body and your back straight. Usually worn on the right arm. Only really useful for advanced jumpers.

9 BAREFOOT SKIING

**BY WORLD CHAMPION,
MIKE SEIPEL**

Ever since Jesus stepped out on the Sea of Galilee nearly 2,000 years ago, man has sought the ability to walk on water. Daredevil Ralph Samuelson came close in 1922 when he strapped two one-dollar pine boards to his feet and invented the sport of waterskiing. Soon he was putting on shows, jumping over ramps and skiing on just one ski. With these rapid advances, it was inevitable that someone sooner or later would try waterskiing without skis. And when they did, just over 40 years ago, the exciting sport of barefoot waterskiing was born. Now barefooters can jump, perform tricks, do deepwater starts and slalom – all without skis. It's the nearest mere mortals will come to walking on water, but the feeling of skimming across lakes on bare feet at 30–45 m.p.h. is heavenly. And it does not hurt!

The first barefooter was a skinny 16-year-old called Asbury Garnett Hancock. He succeeded in barefooting across Florida's Lake Howard, Winter Haven, in 1947. He had seen keen waterskier Chuck Sligh having fun with some novel 12-inch long shoe skis – two size 9 sneakers nailed to short planks of wood. Sligh, from Holland, Michigan, USA, was on holiday in Winter Haven and preparing for a tournament at Cypress Gardens. He suggested to the intrigued Hancock that he should have a go, and pulled him around the lake behind his 16 ft Chris Craft. Hancock took to the shoe skis so easily that

Sligh and his friend William Telling said Hancock could probably ski on his bare feet. Hancock thought they were joking. Then, he agreed to give it a try. He pulled out to the left, took his right foot out of the back binding, put his foot in the water (toes up), transferred his weight to his bare foot, and eventually kicked off the ski. Hancock says he had trouble getting out of the binding. 'On the first few tries, getting out of the binder proved to be a problem, so I got up on one ski with my foot on top of the binder and that proved successful,' he recalls. A thrilling new form of waterskiing had been invented.

Since then, barefooting has grown from a spectacular stunt into a thriving, competitive sport, with thousands of barefooters taking part in organised tournaments at regional, national and international level all over the world. The sport is particularly strong in the United States, Australia, New Zealand, Britain and South Africa. World championships have been held every other year since 1978 and one skier, Mike Seipel, has competed in every one, winning the coveted overall title twice – in 1984 and 1986. And Mike only started barefooting in 1970, when he was ten. Since then he has learned and refined the following techniques. They have taken him to the top in a most demanding sport. He learned many of these techniques the hard way – by trial and error. You have it much easier.

Two of the most innovative early barefooters, below *Don Thompson, and* left *Dick Pope Jr.*

THREE STEPS TO LEARNING

1 Learn everything on the boom first.

2 Then practise it using a five-foot extension off the boom.

3 Now you are ready for behind-the-boat instruction.

The boom is fast becoming the most important barefoot teaching aid. When I was learning to barefoot we used a long line, and the falls were hard and frequent. Now you can learn this exhilarating sport without getting your hair wet! If you tuck the boom under your arms while you are learning your first trick, it is almost impossible to fall or hurt yourself. However, I strongly recommend that you learn and perfect all the techniques in this book on a boom first – it will save time in the long run. For those of you not familiar with a boom, it is a strong pole which extends off the side of the boat, parallel to the water. It is an invaluable teaching aid – one of the best coaching innovations, not only for barefooting, but also for waterskiing. It helps you to learn new skills faster and more safely. When you have your arms over the boom, or are holding on to it, you are taking the weight off your feet in the water and allowing yourself to learn at distinctly lower speeds – which means falls, if they happen, are less hard. The boom also gives the new barefooter confidence and eliminates the deadly slack that can plague those learning on a towrope.

Since the boom is extended out to the side of the boat, you do not have to contend with such variables as boat turbulence and wake, either. Another advantage is the nearness of your instructor and the observers in the boat. They can watch you closely and even talk you through a particularly difficult manoeuvre.

The boom is positioned a few feet above the water, giving you an upward pull which lessens the drag and the long, uncomfortable pull through the water on long-line starts. After you learn a manoeuvre on the boom, you should attach a handle with a five-foot rope extension. The disadvantages of learning behind the boat – the wake and the long, hard drag through the water – are still eliminated with the five-foot rope extension, but you can get a more realistic feeling of what you are doing.

The next step is to transfer to behind the boat. It will be much easier, faster and safer to accomplish each skill because the basic feeling and technique has already been learned on the boom. The big difference is more drag and, as a result, more strength and energy is required to do a manoeuvre. When used properly, the boom is a safe, useful learning tool. I urge all the skiers I instruct to follow these steps:

1 Learn any given trick directly on the boom.

2 Go on to a five-foot extension.

3 Now you are ready for behind-the-boat instruction, it should be a breeze.

The boom is not just for learning. I use the boom on- and off-season for very hard training, to stay in shape or just to play around and have a good time. We also use the boom when photographers are in the boat – it provides sharp, close-up angles that would often be impossible behind the boat.

And besides, it is fun to ski or barefoot right alongside the people in the boat.

EQUIPMENT

The boom – as we have already mentioned, a most important teaching device. It makes the learning process more enjoyable, faster, safer and easier. This safe, strong boom will fit any type of boat on the market today.

Wetsuits – these, and the wetsuit shorts, were designed and manufactured specifically for barefoot waterskiing. They have flotation and padding sewn in where needed and will not restrict your arms, legs and body movement. Barefoot falls can be hard and painful, so you need good protection.

Handles – a 15-inch wake slalom, start and turns handle. It is wider than the normal 12-inch waterskiing handle, so it offers the barefooter more balance, in much the same way that a wider stance might help. The clear plastic protectors prevent rope burns and wetsuit chafing.

Rope – different to ordinary waterskiing rope because it is non-stretch and is called Kevlar barefoot line. It has an inner core of Kevlar fibreglass and polypropylene with an outer cover of 12-strand binded polypropylene. This makes the rope non-stretch like cable, safer and provides a smoother ride across the water. It also provides a steadier pull while you are doing the different manoeuvres and tricks. The rope should be 75–85 ft long, including the 5 ft length attached to the handle.

Toe-up harness – this strap is used for doing toe starts – forwards and backwards – and hand skiing. You are not towed by a handle, but by the toe strap, which has padding for comfort.

Neck support – this piece of equipment offers additional support while barefooting backwards and doing advanced manoeuvres, such as 180° turns.

68

Gloves – important because they stop callousing and give you a much stronger grip while doing tricks and manoeuvres.

Drysuit – helps skiers in cold climates to extend their season. A Flo-motion vest and wetsuit shorts should be worn underneath for protection and flotation.

Flip-turn ski – this will help a person learn backward barefooting. It is unique because everything is turned around. You can either come out of the water backwards on this from a deepwater start, or you can come out forwards and do a 180° turn, like a trick skier. You then step off it.

Walk-around step-off ski – can be used for doing front step-offs or back step-offs. It is unique because it does not have any bindings. All it has is black non-skid tape which enables a person to get up forwards and then turn around and get set up in a backward step-off position.

Front step-off ski – probably the best thing to use when you are learning to barefoot (see below.

Boat – the best barefoot boats have plenty of power, produce small wakes and are easy to manoeuvre.

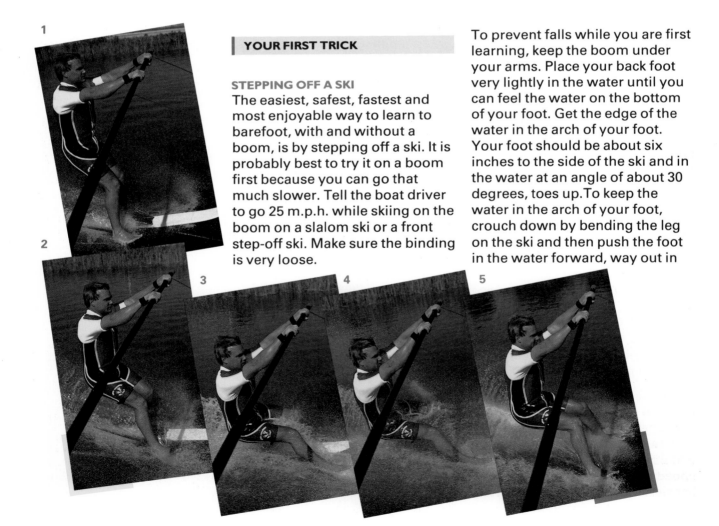

YOUR FIRST TRICK

STEPPING OFF A SKI

The easiest, safest, fastest and most enjoyable way to learn to barefoot, with and without a boom, is by stepping off a ski. It is probably best to try it on a boom first because you can go that much slower. Tell the boat driver to go 25 m.p.h. while skiing on the boom on a slalom ski or a front step-off ski. Make sure the binding is very loose.

To prevent falls while you are first learning, keep the boom under your arms. Place your back foot very lightly in the water until you can feel the water on the bottom of your foot. Get the edge of the water in the arch of your foot. Your foot should be about six inches to the side of the ski and in the water at an angle of about 30 degrees, toes up. To keep the water in the arch of your foot, crouch down by bending the leg on the ski and then push the foot in the water forward, way out in front of the boom about 18 inches in front of your other foot. The boat driver should still be going 25 m.p.h. When you get down in this plant position, bending very low with your bare foot in the water out in front of you and the water in the middle of your foot, you cannot fall. The water has to get above your toes to make you fall. If the water comes up towards your toes, bend your ski leg more and push your bare foot farther forward. Slowly transfer three-quarters of your weight onto your bare foot by leaning your hip, shoulders and whole body over to that side. Lean so much that your ski foot feels like it is just going to fall out of the binding. As the ski comes off, make sure you are keeping the water in the middle of your bare foot. When the ski comes off, do not rush to put your other foot in the water: Put it in cautiously; make sure the water only goes into the arch of the foot.

Once you have mastered this, try it while you are holding on to the boom with your arms extended. Once you can successfully step off every time, put a short rope on the boom and try again. Your feet should be shoulder width apart; your knees bent; feet at an angle of about 30 degrees; toes up; arms comfortably straight with handle at waist level; shoulders slightly behind hips; and head up. The only difference between holding on to the boom and using a short rope extension is that you have to concentrate much harder on balance, and the boat will need to go slightly faster. To figure out your speed as you go into the low plant position, take your weight in pounds, divide it by 10 and add 20. For example, if you weigh 150 lbs, divide by 10 to get 15 and add 20 to give you a barefoot speed of 35 m.p.h. Once the boat accelerates to this speed, and you are sure you are low enough to

keep the water in the middle of your foot, slowly follow through as you have learned directly on the boom.

When you first put your foot in the water on the long rope, start at 30 m.p.h. Position yourself outside the wake so that you are in the curl of it, with your bare foot in the water banking up against the wake. If you are planting your right foot, you should be on the left side of the wake. The water is smoother in this 'curl'. As you go into the low plant position, have the boat accelerate up to the speed you have figured out with the formula, and follow the exact steps learned on the boom. Remember, balance and getting down to the water are very important behind the boat. Stay down low and concentrate on your balance. You are now barefooting – get used to the feeling. Great, isn't it?

KNEEBOARD START

If you do not have a front step-off ski, you can use a kneeboard. The kneeboard start is one of the easiest and safest ways to learn to barefoot, especially when a boom is not available. To learn this start you will need 100 ft of non-stretch Kevlar rope, water-tight wetsuit shorts, a life-jacket or a barefoot suit and a kneeboard.

The first part of the kneeboard start is balance – you must be able to sit up securely in the middle front of the board. Practise by sitting upright in the water, with your legs hanging off the side, as if you were riding a horse. Once you have mastered this, have your observer bring the handle to you. Use your legs and feet to hold yourself in place while you are being pulled out of the water. As the boat slowly accelerates up to 15 m.p.h., lean back so the front of the board stays out of the water. Lift your legs out of the water in front of you. At 15 m.p.h., you should be riding smoothly. If you bounce, slide yourself forward until it stops. Once you are riding smoothly, put your heels in the water very lightly and slowly. Your feet should make a 30–45-degree – or slightly flatter – angle with the surface of the water. Make sure you do not put them in hard or straight up against the water. Your knees should be bent at a 90-degree angle. Once you can feel the water on your feet, and the water's edge is hitting the arch of your foot, have the boat accelerate to your barefoot speed (dividing your body weight in pounds by 10 and adding 20). Don't get anxious and stand up too quickly. Relax and stay in position, sitting on the board. Do not pull in the handle with your arms. If you wait until the boat gets up to speed, the board will slowly slide out from under you as you smoothly plant your feet and stand up. If you do not want to fall, it is as simple as this: keep the water's edge at the arch of your feet by sitting low to the water. If spray is in your face, point your toes inward towards each other and keep your knees bent.

1

2

3

SIMPLE STARTS

FORWARD DEEPWATER START

The next trick learned in barefoot waterskiing is the forward deepwater start. Lie in the water with both feet wrapped over the rope. Take a deep breath and throw your head back. This will be the signal for the boat driver to take off. As the boat takes off, straighten your legs and push down on the rope with your feet so your body becomes very arched. Lay your head way back in the water and get your hips very high in the air by pushing down on the rope with your feet. That way your body acts like a giant ski and you will surface very quickly.

After you surface, very slowly sit up and ride on the pivot point (the butt pad of your wetsuit). Wait for the boat to pick up speed, then take your feet off the rope, bend your knees and set your feet in the water very, very slowly and lightly. This will raise you into the forward barefoot position. Keep the handle close to your stomach throughout. Let the boat pull you up.

1

2

3

4

5

6

7

TUMBLETURN START

The next tricks learned are the tumbleturn start and tumbleturn recovery.

First, you will learn the tumbleturn start. The boat will slowly accelerate, bringing you out of the water on your elbows and knees. Once you get up to a speed of about 25 m.p.h. roll onto your back. Once you are on your back there is only one thing you have to do to complete a tumbleturn spin – pull the handle from over your head around to your hip.

As you watch a tumbleturn, it

1

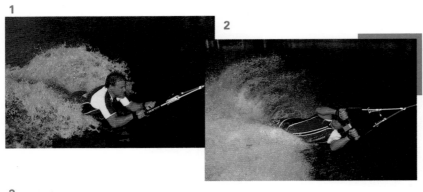

2

3

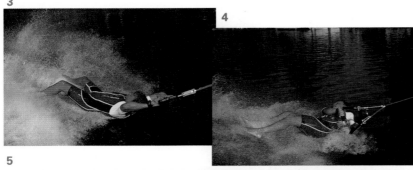

4

5

6

7

8

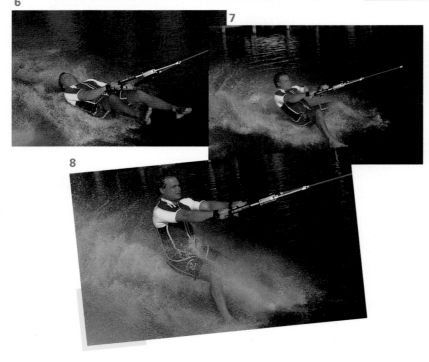

looks like the skier has a lot to do and a lot to think about but, in fact, all he/she is doing is taking the handle from over the head and around the side towards the hip. Once the handle touches the hip, the boat will bring the skier's feet around in front of him or her. Now the skier is in the forward deepwater start position and can stand up by bending the knees and placing the feet very slowly and lightly in the water.

Once you have mastered the tumbleturn start, you can learn the tumbleturn recovery, where you barefoot along, do a tumbleturn, stand up again and barefoot away. While you are barefooting along, crouch down by bending your knees and get very low to the water. Then, let your feet go out to one side and, at the same time, lean your head and shoulders back. The handle will pass up at forehead level and then all you must think about is bringing that handle out and down to your hip. As you touch your hip with the handle, the boat will bring your feet around in front of you. Remember to keep your knees bent and set your feet in the water extra slowly and lightly – don't jam them in. Then, rise up smoothly to the forward barefoot position: toes up, feet shoulder width apart, legs bent, arms relaxed, handle at waist level and shoulders slightly behind hips.

The only other thing I could tell you to improve your tumbleturn is that once you get on your back with the handle by your head, you should try to keep your knees tilted away from the direction of the spin. That is, try to keep the leading edge – your hip and right leg if you are spinning clockwise – out of the water. Turning your head and looking to the hip that is in the water will help.

74

MORE TRICKS

ONE-FOOT TRICKS

The next tricks to learn are the forward one foot and forward toehold. It does not take a great deal of skill to do a clean one foot – just concentration. As you are barefooting along in the two-foot position, bring your feet close together. If you are going to ski on your left foot, lean your hips, shoulders and whole body over to the left, and as you pick up the right foot, concentrate on the foot that is in the water. Make sure the water is not climbing up over your toes before you take your other heel completely out of the water. If the water is climbing up over your toes, lower your body by bending your knee. Then, hunch forward for the perfect one-foot position.

Practise skiing on one foot, and move the free foot to the right and left. Once you can do this, and do deep knee bends on the leg in the water without getting spray in your face, you can learn the forward toehold. When you are doing this trick, the main thing to think about is doing a good, comfortable one foot. Bring your feet together. If you are going to ski on your left foot, lean your hips, shoulders and whole body over to the left and, as you pick up your right foot, make sure the water is not getting up over your left toes. If it is climbing up towards your toes, by lowering your body and staying hunched forward, you will be able to stop that from happening. Once you get in the forward one-foot position, with no spray in your

face and riding in total control, you can lower the toe strap securely onto your free foot. Stay upright and forward and stay leaning over to your left. Now let go of the handle. Do this fairly quickly, because when you have both hands on the handle and one foot in the strap you have very little balance. You no longer have your foot or hands to help you balance, so once you have your foot deep in the strap, release straightaway and get your arms out to the side for balance. Keep thinking about where the water's edge is, and stay hunched forward and leaning over to your left. It is the same technique for right and left one foots and toeholds.

TEETH AND NECK HOLDS

Once you have perfected your one foots and toeholds, you can learn teeth and neck holds. For these tricks, you will need a handle with a teeth strap and plastic stiffeners, instead of the normal loose rope. The stiffeners give the handle a wide opening, so that it can come off your head easily in a fall.

A teeth hold is done by placing the teeth piece way back on to your molars while you are barefooting. Get a good firm bite. At first do the trick while you are riding on two feet, and then, after you get comfortable, you can go on to the one foot. Do it as you would do a normal one foot, but, because the pull is from a much higher position on the body, you have to concentrate on staying very low and leaning back.

The neck hold, where you put the handle over your head, is similar to the teeth hold. First, you practise it while barefooting on two feet, and then, once you become comfortable, you can do the one foots. Remember to lean back and get low. Pull the handle over your head to the back of your neck by gripping the stiffeners at the end closest to the boat.

BACKWARD BAREFOOTING

Once these forward tricks have been perfected, you can go on to learn the exciting art of backward barefooting. One way to learn backward barefooting is on a backward step-off or flip-turn ski. Sit on the boom, holding it with your palms facing up – your weight should be on the boom and the ski just resting on the surface of the water. After the boat has accelerated slowly to about 25 m.p.h., slowly transfer your weight to the ski by rolling off the boom. Do it slowly until you are standing on the ski.

Because you are holding directly onto the boom, you will be able to learn this trick at a much slower and safer speed, and the boom will give you a tremendous amount of confidence as well as balance. Take your time getting comfortable and riding the ski backwards. Lift your back foot into the air, then place it back on the ski. Then, practise crouching down and standing up. When you are ready, lift your back foot off the ski and place it very lightly in the water, close to the ski. Your foot should be almost flat. Don't point your toes. Once you get the feeling of the water on the bottom of your foot and you are confident that the water is not going to get above your heel, crouch down and push that bare foot forward (behind you) until you get into what we call the 'track start' or backward barefoot plant position. Ride this position and get used to it. Once you know the water is not going to get above your heel, lean your hips, shoulders and whole body over your plant foot, and pick up the heel on the ski high up and away from the ski. Do not rush placing this foot in the water after the ski releases – with your plant foot you are automatically doing a one foot.

1

2

78

3

4

5

6

7

8

BACKWARD DEEPWATER START

The next thing to learn is the backward deepwater start. There are three basic steps to this start.

1 Lie in the water on your stomach with one foot over the rope and the handle on your backside, arms out straight. Grip the handle with palms up, knuckles down.

2 As the boat takes off, take a deep breath and straighten your legs. When the boat reaches 10–12 m.p.h., you will be able to breathe easily and should not be bouncing. Take your foot off the rope and ride on your cup (or pelvis) and inner thighs.

3 Once you are clearly going across the water without bouncing, you can place your feet in the water and stand up. To stand up, spread your legs very, very wide and cock your feet up towards your body and outwards (towards the sides of the lake or river). Now, when you place your feet in the water lightly, they will stay there. This phase is by far the most important. Most people, as they set their feet in the water, tend to resist or push against the water with the balls of their feet or with their toes. But your feet cannot glide across the surface of the water that way. They will bounce in and out, or spear right through the water, so make sure you get your feet very wide and that you stay relaxed and let the water push your feet flat. Once you get your feet firmly in the water, and the boat driver can see that your feet are firmly in the water, he can slowly accelerate you up to your normal back barefoot speed of about 35 m.p.h. When you feel the acceleration, stand up by pressing down on your chest and chin. Pulling in on the handle, or fighting in any way, will not get you anywhere. Just push down against the water with your chest and chin and lift your backside into the back barefoot position. As you stand up, you will be able to bring your feet closer together and bend your knees. The correct back barefoot position is knees bent, body bent forwards at the waist, feet comfortably close together, chin up and head up looking out to the horizon.

BACK ONE FOOTS

Once you have perfected the back two foot, you can learn your back one foots, which are similar to the forward one foots. There is not much technique involved. As you are back barefooting, bring your feet together. If you are going to ski on your right foot, lean your hips, shoulders and whole body over to your right, and as you pick up on your left foot make sure that the water line is not going to get above your heel. If you leave your left toes just touching the water, until you are sure your right heel will not sink, you can prevent many falls. The technique is the same if you are going to ski on your left foot – feet together, lean to your left, and as you pick up on your right foot, concentrate on the foot that is going to stay in the water. Make sure the water is not going to get above your heel. If you think it is, bend forward more and bend your skiing leg more to keep your heel from catching.

BACK TO FRONT

The next trick you should learn is the back to front. The key to this trick is getting in the correct set-up position. It is even worth taking a day or so to learn and become comfortable with this position – in fact, you should not even try to turn from back to front until you are very comfortable riding backwards in the set-up position.

To set up while skiing backwards, bring your feet together, bend your knees and put your heels down as low to the water as possible without catching. Your arms should be straight, with your upper body broken at the waist, so your chest is low. Now lift your head and arch your shoulders up so you are looking out. To do the back to front from this position, don't try to turn forwards. Don't even give in and let the boat turn you around. What you have to do to make a smooth back to front is pin the arm that is going to keep hold of the handle into the hip, so it cannot come off your hip when you are pulled around. Press your arm hard into your hip and then let go with the other hand. Resist the boat. Don't let it turn you around. You cannot stay backward as you hold your set-up position, but don't try to turn or give in to the boat and let it pull

you around. Instead, try to ski one hand backwards. If you hold the back to front set-up position, the boat will turn you smoothly to the front. As it does, lean your shoulders back and lean over to the side opposite the hand holding the handle to counteract the boat pulling on your arm and making you tip over to the side. If you are getting pulled forward after the turn, try to keep your shoulders back. If you get pulled and tip to one side after the turn, lean to the opposite side you are holding the handle with.

ADVANCED TRICKS

FRONT TO BACK

It is probably easier to learn this trick with a pair of shoe skis on. You get up on these in the same way as you would on a forward deepwater start – the boat pulling you at about 20–25 m.p.h. For a very big person, it would be 28 m.p.h. maximum. At 25 m.p.h. the falls are less hard and it is easier to perfect good technique and get the feeling for the whole trick. The shoe skis also mean you can repeat the trick more often in one session, which teaches you muscle memory and strengthens the muscles needed when you come to turn on your feet. I find my basic turn is turning to my left, because my left foot is my strong foot. For you it may be turning to the right. You start your turn by bringing your feet comfortably close together, and as you bend down, you turn the handle up so it is almost vertical – the hand of your stronger side should be highest. So, if I am going to turn to my left, my left hand will go higher than my right hand. I'd then raise up, and that would put me into a rotation, turning most heavily on my left foot. I'd let go with my left hand, spin to the backward barefoot position and grab the handle again with my left hand. Think about raising and turning slowly by putting your butt up to the handle, and think

1

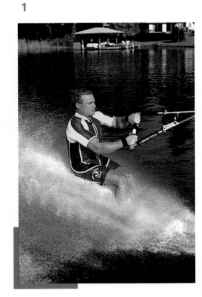

2

3

4

about getting the handle as fast as you can, keeping your chest low and head up.

The reverse of this trick is done with a completely different technique. To initiate the turn on a reverse front to back; bend down, let the handle out, and let your shoulders go forward. As you rise up, start the turn by pulling in on the handle with your stronger side hand, let go with the other hand and step behind your stronger foot through the spray. Again, think about raising up and turning slow by putting your butt up to the handle, keeping your feet close together and try to get the handle as soon as possible. Keep your chest low and head up.

So, basically, there are two ways to do a front to back. If you are stepping in front of your stronger foot, you want to cock the handle as you bend down. To turn the other way, let the handle out, crouch down for your 'unweight' and as you take the weight off the water, pull in very hard with your stronger hand as your weaker foot steps behind the other one. These techniques and methods should come very naturally to you once you start using shoe skis. The best thing to do is to go out on a pair of shoe skis and determine which way you turn most comfortably, and which foot has the most weight on it when you are doing the turn. Once you find this out, you can use the above techniques to complete your turn more effectively. Start out each run on shoe skis at 25 m.p.h. to build up a rhythm. Then start doing them at slower speeds – all the way down to 16–18 m.p.h. if you weigh 175–200 lbs, or 14–16 m.p.h. if you weigh 150–175 lbs. When you can do as many as you want at your slowest speed, then take off the shoe skis. You should have the muscle memory and strength to make it on your bare feet.

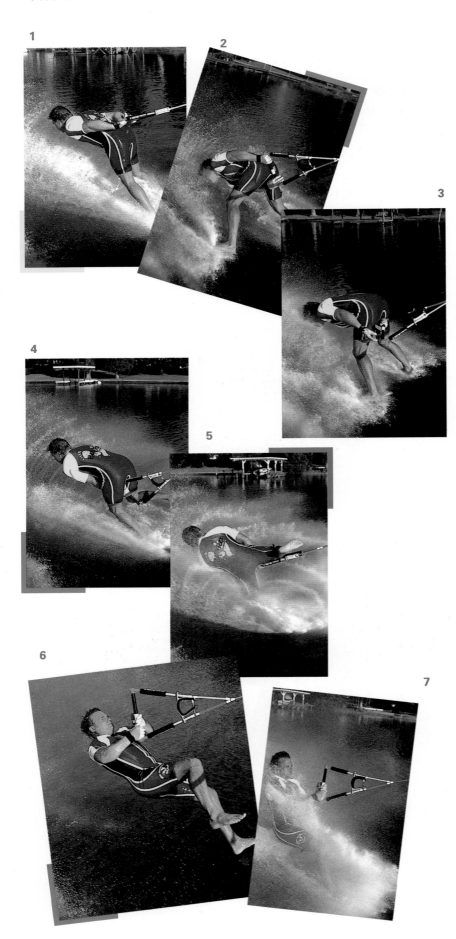

82

LINE STEP BACK TO FRONT

The next trick to learn is the line step back to front. Here again, practise on shoe skis first. In fact, I recommend you use shoe skis to learn all your surface turns. Remember, you will have a lot of spray and feel you are sinking when you slow down. Use small shoe skis – even after you make the trick on your feet, go back and finish with workouts on shoe skis for six months to build strength.

To do a line step back to front, you start in the backward barefoot position and then spread your legs very, very wide. Now slowly let go of the handle with one hand, bring this hand in front of you and re-grab the handle from between your legs. Let go with the other hand. Once you get the handle down between your legs, bring your feet comfortably close together and learn how to ride in this position. Don't worry about getting into the forward position until you become very comfortable riding in the back barefoot position with the rope down between your legs. The next step is to transfer up to 90 per cent of your weight to your strong foot. I recommend you have one hand on the handle and one hand in the air for balance. Once you can ride back barefoot with 90 per cent of your weight on your strong foot and the rope down between your legs, you can then go for the line step back to front, by giving a very small unweight and coming to the forward position, your weaker foot stepping over the line. If your strong foot is your left foot, hold the handle with your right hand and step over the line with your right foot. If your strong foot is your right foot, you hang on with your left hand as you come to the forward position.

TURNS

Once the front to back and the back to front are perfected, the 360 is quite an easy trick to learn. All you have to do is concentrate on completing a smooth front to back, and then, once you get to the back barefoot position, do a smooth back to front. It is important to do a smooth front to back with no extra effort – without throwing it any harder – and after you get your hand on the handle in the back barefoot position, come to the forward position. You have done two smooth 180s, or a 360.

Other multiple turns that evolve from learning the clean, basic front to back and the clean, basic back to front are:

- back to backs – where you do a back to front, and as soon as you get the handle, rotate in a smooth front to back without stopping.

- 540s to the front and to the back, which have to be done clearly without hesitation.

- 720s to the back and 720s to the front – the most advanced of the multiple turns and very, very difficult to judge.

1

2

3

4

5

6

7

8

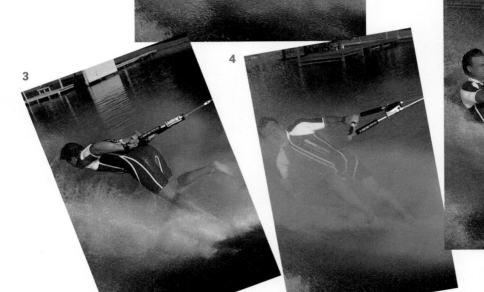

ONE-FOOT TURNS

Another variation of the surface turns are the one-foot turns. One foot turns are surface turns from front to back and back to front supported by one foot only. They are performed in exactly the same way as the two-foot turns, but on your strong foot only. Practise rotating from front to back and from back to front. Once you have mastered these, try to do a smooth one-foot 360, which is the most advanced trick done on one foot.

LINE STEP FRONT TO BACK

The next trick learned is a line step front to back. Very few competitors do this trick, because it is scored quite low for its difficulty. You should be able to do a good one-foot turn before learning the line step front to back. The most important thing to remember when doing this trick is to keep your legs very close together until you have turned backwards – then you reach over the rope with your weaker leg. If you were to reach over the rope while you were turning, your foot could drop into the handle or you could do a very bad split and pull a groin muscle. By rotating with your legs together and then reaching your foot over the rope very smooothly and instantly, you'll be able to do a safe line step from front to back. One other tip for this trick is to hold the handle at one end with both hands together. Grip the left side of the handle if you are going to turn to the left.

84

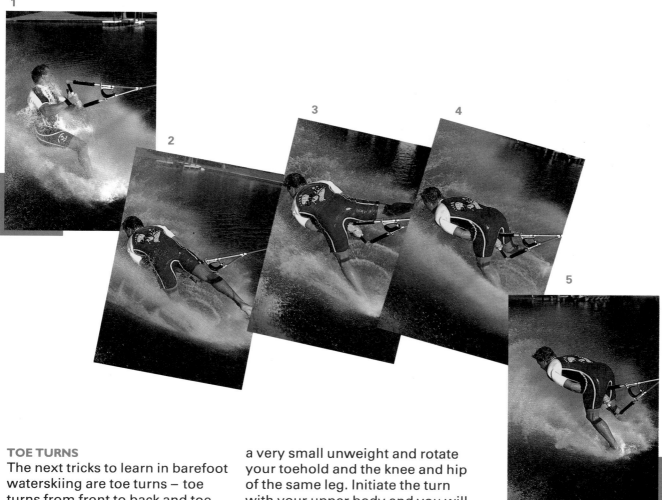

TOE TURNS

The next tricks to learn in barefoot waterskiing are toe turns – toe turns from front to back and toe turns from back to front.

It is very important to be able to ride a front toehold and back toehold in total control. Once both tricks are learned and perfected, a toe front to back can be quite easy. As you are barefooting along in the front toehold position, all you have to do is give a very small unweight and rotate your toehold and the knee and hip of the same leg. Initiate the turn with your upper body and you will be able to turn smoothly into the back toehold position. There is not a great deal of technique to this trick – basically, stay quite relaxed and comfortable, and keep the leg of the foot that is in the water slightly bent. Before you turn from front to back, make sure your foot is deep into the strap.

That will help when you come to do the toe back to front. Once you have turned backwards and become steady, do not rush – just turn forward from the back toe position and bend the knee of the foot in the water right up to your stomach. You will sit softer if you try to land on the lower part of your back. As quickly as possible, lean over to the side of the foot going into the water as you rock forward and place your foot in the water. Also, it helps not only to lean towards the side of the foot going into the water, but to grab way up by the ankle of the foot in the strap with your hand. Remember this is the ankle in the strap, and push off the water with the hand on the same side as the foot going into the water. This will put you in the normal toehold position. If your foot pops out of the water after you set it in, place your foot in closer to your body until your foot stays in the water. If you get halfway and fall back, grab further up on your ankle next time.

All surface turns, one-foot turns and toehold turns can be done in reverse for extra points.

ADVANCED START METHODS

FRONT TOE-UP

One of the amazing start methods that top pro skiers use to start their trick runs is the front toe-up. The easiest way to learn this is to ride along in a front toehold position and grab the ankle of the leg that is in the toe strap with the hand that is on the same side, i.e. with your right hand if your right leg is in the toe strap. Now, smoothly sit on the water by bending your knee and putting your free hand on the water first. What you have done is a negative (i.e. you have learned the trick in reverse). You have actually done the toe-up but in the reverse direction. This will give you a tremendous amount of confidence and help you to feel the technique needed to do a toe-up. Once you can sit down smoothly, there is not much technique needed to come back up. All you have to do, as you are riding along on your backside in total control, is grab your ankle, lean over your free leg, put your free hand on the water and, quite relaxed, give a good hard rock forward. By sitting back a little and rocking forward, and then – most importantly – putting your skiing foot in the water very, very hard, you will get up. Don't just push that foot slowly into the water – rock forward and thrust it in. Don't push that foot into the water as hard as you think you have to in order to stand up, press that foot into the water as hard as you can. At the same time, push off the water with the hand on the water and keep grabbing under the ankle with your hand. This will help you stay forward. The more you push off the water, the easier it is to get up.

You may think you will push your foot through the surface of the water but that won't happen –

there's no one standing there pushing down on your head or shoulder. The only possible thing that can happen is that as you place your foot in the water, it may skip out. All you have to do to take care of that is place your foot in a bit closer to your body. The reason your foot is popping out is because it is placed too far out in front of you instead of close underneath your body.

1

2

3

4

6

5

BACK TOE-UP

Another advanced start method is the back toe-up. Prerequisite to a back toe-up is a good strong back toehold. Once you can ride a good strong back toehold, you start in the water face down with your foot in the strap. As the boat takes off, arch your body and press your hips down into the water. After the boat accelerates up to 10 m.p.h., place your skiing foot as close to the other foot in the strap as you can, and as you place it in the water, let the foot come underneath you and let your backside raise up into the air. You must stay very relaxed, it doesn't take much energy – the boat will pull you into position. All you need to do is relax and follow that pull. The most important thing is to keep the foot going in the water in position, with the toe pointed back in the direction of your body. Relax the foot and let the water push the top of your foot back up towards your shin.

BACK DEEP TO ONE

The things to remember when you are doing the back deep to one are to place the foot in directly underneath the rope and to hang on extra tight. Your body will stay fairly straight as you lift up whereas in a back deep to two your backside and then your chest, come up out of the water. Remember to ride in total control on your hips at 30 m.p.h. By trying to break the handle over your lower back, rolling your shoulders down and lifting up your thighs with straight legs, you will get a smooth ride on your hips.

1

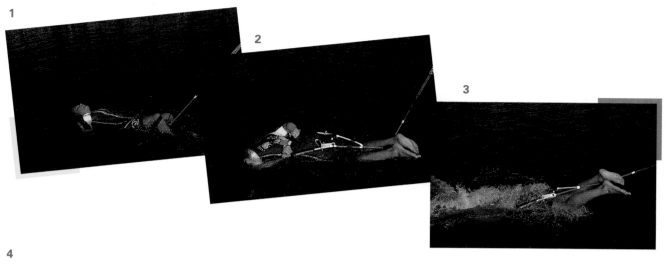

2

3

4

5

6

FRONT ONE-FOOT STAND UP

The front one-foot stand up is where you ride up from a deepwater start and stand up on one foot – your strong foot. You can also do your tumble recoveries and your tumble up start to one foot, to score extra points. The key is riding in total control, sitting on the water with your feet in the air and knees bent. Once you have control, lean towards your skiing foot as you put your foot in the water and rock forward to stand.

WAKE SLALOM

Another event in barefoot waterskiing is wake slalom. Wake slalom is where a barefooter crosses back and forth across the wake, instead of around buoys, as you do in normal slalom skiing. Every boat has a wake behind it and the skier has to cross the wake completely. After completing the cross, you turn, switch directions and cross back. In competition, you have 15 seconds to do as many crosses as you can. Professional or top skiers do the wake crosses on one foot.

To do a wake crossing, you need to start in a strong forward barefoot position. If I want to go to my right, I take my outside foot – or my left foot – and start pushing pressure, or driving it towards the boat. As you drive it towards the boat, pick up on your inside foot a little, and as you cross through the wake, continue to keep that pressure, or that drive, towards the boat. Continue to keep that outside foot you are driving with beneath the rope until you complete the cross, then switch back, turn and head to your left. To head back, it is the same thing, except that your right foot is your outside foot. Drive that right foot forward. As you drive it forward, pick up the left foot – or inside foot – a little. As you continue to cross the wake, make sure that you continue that drive, and that your outside foot – the one you are driving with – is underneath the rope. To go faster, just turn the foot you are pushing on, so that your toes are pointed more in the direction you are going. There are two important things to remember: you are driving with your outside foot, or pushing pressure towards the boat with your outside foot, while picking up on your inside foot; and you should always keep your outside foot underneath the rope as you turn it, to get more speed.

For competitions, you have to wake slalom backwards, too. The top skiers do their wake crossings backwards on one foot. To begin backwards barefoot wake crossing, start in a strong back barefoot position. Then it is the same thing as forward. If you want to head towards your left, take your right foot – or outside foot – and start pushing it, or driving it, towards the boat. At the same time, lighten up on your inside foot and as you drive that right foot forward, it will move underneath the rope automatically. Continue to drive that foot towards the boat throughout the entire cross. Once you have completely crossed the wake, head back to the right. Your outside foot will be your left foot, so drive your left foot towards the boat. It will automatically move under the rope. As you drive hard on it, pick up on that right foot slightly and then you will be crossing back to your right. By using this method of learning wake slalom, you will be able to move right into forward and backwards one-foot wake crossings just by picking up more and more on that inside foot as you gain more confidence. To go faster, just turn the foot you are pushing on, so the heel is aiming more in the direction you are going.

There are three basic things to remember in wake slalom: your outside foot should be pushed towards the boat and underneath the rope, your inside foot should be picked up slightly, and then one foot should be picked up clearly for the judges. Also, to go faster, turn the foot you are pushing on in the direction you are going more and more.

Wake crossing backwards on one foot – drive the foot in the water towards the boat.

JUMPING

To learn how to barefoot jump safely, you should be very, very strong on your feet. You should be able to do one foots, toeholds, teeth and neck, teeth and neck one foots, and be able to cross the wake. If you are able to do all these things, you are ready to attempt barefoot jumping safely. Make sure the water is glass smooth when you barefoot jump – you do not want to risk catching a toe in the rough water.

Three things to remember to land your first jump:

1 Know where that water's edge is on your feet and keep your toes up.

2 Line up. As the driver approaches the jump, he/she sets up with the jump 10–12 ft out to his/her right, which means you actually have to cut out from the wake of the boat to line up with the jump.

3 Most importantly, if you are going to land that jump after you go over the ramp, hang on to that handle. The landings can be hard and if you are not thinking of hanging on, which you are not normally the first couple of times, you forget to hang on and the handle pops out of your hand when you hit the water.

To recap
1 Toes up and know where the water's edge is on the bottom of your feet.
2 Line up – cut out to the right, because that's where the jump is going to be, and set up to go over the ramp.
3 Hang on.

As you approach the ramp, you want to be in a chair position, with your knees bent at about a 60-degree angle. As you come up to

1

2

3

4

5

6

7

8

9

10

11

the jump, don't pull in. Instead, just slowly rise when you are about five feet from it. This will stop your backside from hitting the jump. It's not a spring – you are just keeping your butt from hitting the jump. Don't straighten your legs completely – they will need to absorb a little shock when you hit the ramp. To go longer, you first have to be able to jump short distances feet to feet. Learn on the boom with no rope. When you can go over the jump, and your feet do not slip out forwards at all, then add a raise up. Perfect time to raise up is about two to five feet out, so that you are still raising on the jump and, at the top of the jump, you are completely standing. Once you learn to raise with this perfect timing, and at the same time stop your feet from slipping forward, you will get your longest jumps.

TIPS FOR BOAT DRIVERS

The speeds given in this chapter are generally for an average weight skier of 150 lbs learning on a boom. For a 200 lb skier add about 5 m.p.h. For a light skier of about 100 lb, subtract 5 m.p.h. The base speed is 35 to 37 m.p.h. for a 150 pounder. Add 5–7 m.p.h. for one foot tricks – that is, tow the skier at 40–42 m.p.h. whenever he/she is doing tricks on one foot. Add another 3 m.p.h. if the skier is performing these tricks on a long rope.

Skier's weight	Normal speed long line	One foot tricks	Forwards on boom	Backwards on boom	Backwards on long line
100 lb	30 mph	35–37 mph	27 mph	23 mph	26 mph
150 lb	35 mph	40–42 mph	32 mph	28 mph	31 mph
200 lb	40 mph	45–47 mph	37 mph	33 mph	36 mph

Guide to barefoot skiing speeds

SKI RACING

BY WORLD CHAMPION, STEVE MOORE MBE

10

Steve Moore has waterskied across Lake Windermere, in England's Lake District, at speeds in excess of 100 miles an hour. And that was just four years after seeing his first ski racing event. In 1983, the self-employed car body repairer tried to break the world waterski speed record. After smashing the 101 m.p.h. record on the first of the two mandatory kilometre-long stretches, he fell on the second leg when he was doing about 115 m.p.h. He cartwheeled through the air for an estimated 500 feet, and escaped with just bad bruises and torn knee ligaments.

'They were the most terrifying moments of my life. I was lucky,' he recalls. But, he says to would-be champions, 'If you're not falling, you're not learning. You learn by your mistakes. So keep trying, and don't get disheartened when you fall.'

His boat driver, brother-in-law Jim Cramphorn, says: 'He's a fearless sort of fella. He's not frightened of the speed and the falls, and he has had some very fast and hard falls. He's always wanted to just go out on the water and race to win. Initially, we didn't have the experience to do that, but none the less had a lot of fun trying. He'd have a brilliant half race and then have a fall, and it was all over. But, eventually, you get enough experience, stop falling and start winning.'

His combination of skill and courage, backed by a good team, have helped him to win five British Championships, four European gold medals, the 1986 World Cup and 1987 World Championships.

Ski racing is fast and exciting and, with the element of danger, is a real crowd puller. The sight of 20–60 highly tuned and powerful ski boats pulling skiers at speeds sometimes over 80 m.p.h. around an inland or coastal course is breathtaking.

Unlike barefoot and tournament skiing, ski racing is a team sport, where skier, driver and observer are all important and, when a certain understanding is achieved between the three, racing becomes an enjoyable and often successful sport. The job of the driver is to steer the team through the race, picking the best lines along the straights, around the corners, and past the slower boats. The driver not only has to watch out for his/her team but also the other teams, bearing in mind that he/she is driving a potentially lethal weapon. The driver has to have a good knowledge of boats and how they will handle in different waters at speed; the driver's eyes must be watching for other skiers who may have fallen, as well as watching for where the competition is. The speed of the race will sometimes be chosen by the driver, who will be guided by the speeds of the teams you are racing. The driving must be consistent at all times, and by this I mean that the speed must be steady, and when asked to slow down or speed up, the driver must do this gently but quickly and, at all times, must keep the ski line tight. Many a skier has fallen when the driver has slowed down too quickly – the skier gets a slack line and this can prove fatal. When a team has been together for a while, the driver will learn how his/her skier will react to different types of water, and how quickly the skier will be able to go.

The driver will be constantly relying on information from the observer about the skier's form on that particular day, and on any team coming up behind to challenge. The observer's job is to watch the skier very carefully. The observer must learn to tell the difference between a skier having a bad moment and the style in which he/she skis. Some skiers look 'untidy', they look likely to fall, even if they say they are comfortable in this style. This type of skier will be an observer's nightmare and make the job even harder than it already is. The observer is the link person between skier and driver, telling the driver to go faster or slower when the skier has signalled for a different speed. The observer will be watching for any challenge from behind and, if there is, will instruct the driver to go faster if he/or she thinks the skier is capable. When an observer has been with a skier and driver for a period of time, he/she will learn how they will react to different situations and will in turn react to keep the team in the best position. After a time, the observer will see how the skier skis, and will often be able to tell the driver to slow down in the event of any difficulties experienced before the skier has had time to signal directly. The same applies to the driver, who will learn to react to the fidgets and movements of the observer when the skier is in trouble, sometimes before being signalled. The observer, like the driver, will be watching other teams as well as keeping a keen eye on his/her skier. The job is to keep the skier up for the complete race and to watch for any signs of tiredness, where speeds will be adjusted accordingly. The observer will inform the driver when coming into turns of boats, either on the inside or outside, or, if the driver takes a turn too tight and puts their skier in danger, tell the driver to adjust the line, if at all possible.

There are no set signals for ski racing. Each team will devise their own to suit themselves. The best advice is to keep the signals simple, and have them already worked out before going onto the water. One of the most confusing things for a skier is to be signalled by an observer, using a sign not used before. The skier will waste valuable time working out what the observer has signalled, when he/she should be concentrating on skiing. The skier's main aim is to ski the race as quickly as possible without falling off, and, of course, to win the race. The skier must place complete trust in the crew – this will only come when he/she is confident that they are helping the skier to do his/her job. One of the biggest battles for a skier is learning to concentrate for the duration of the race – once this is achieved the rest is down to skill, technique, stamina, determination, the crew, and a little bit of luck. I cannot stress too strongly that concentration is a large part of the success of a good ski racer. Any lapse in concentration can lead to falls and sometimes injury.

To get started in ski racing, it is best to contact your national ski association (e.g. British Water Ski Federation, American Water Ski Association) for a list of ski race clubs in your area. They will send you the rules and regulations on ski racing and details on how to qualify for your racing permits. It is best to join a ski racing club because they will help you to improve. Most clubs organise their own club and regional races, which is the best way to learn ski racing and gain experience before entering into the national series.

There are two main classes – ladies and senior men, then,

depending on your age, there are classes for dauphins (under 15 years), juniors (under 18 years), and veterans (over 35 years). As with most other sports, it is sometimes best to start at an early age, but not necessary to reach a high level. Men's races are usually for an hour and a lap; women and youngsters race for 45 minutes plus a lap.

There are four formulae, with boat length and engine size deciding in which formula the teams qualify:

- Formula 1: 21 foot boat – 3001 to 8200 cc
- Formula 2: 21 foot boat – 2001 to 3000 cc
- Formula 3: 18 foot boat – 1301 to 2000 cc
- Formula 4: 16 foot boat – up to 1300 cc

Depending on which formula you choose, it can become an expensive sport and so sponsorship is always welcome to help meet costs. A formula 1 twin-engined rig, plus trailer, can cost well over £20,000, with annual running costs in excess of £5,000. At the other end of the scale, a 16 ft boat with a 90 h.p. outboard might cost around £6,000 and, if it

takes part in the formula 4 series, annual expenditure could be about £1,000, barring breakages. In addition to this, a skier could easily spend £750 on equipment. The skier's equipment consists of a good strong lifejacket (which will protect the body if a hard fall is sustained), a ski helmet (which will not fly off when a fall occurs), ski goggles (normally snow ski or motor cross goggles are the best design to stop salt, spray, and wind while going at speed across the water). It is always advisable to wear a wetsuit for protection. It does not necessarily need to be a full suit, it is really down to personal preference. Some are available with built-in buoyancy. Gloves are often a good idea for protection and grip. The ski line should be of a good quality, and care must be taken to ensure it does not have any faults in it, as it can sometimes break under stress. It is a must to always carry a spare line in the event of anything happening to your main line – i.e. if it breaks or if a fall is sustained and, while the boat is turning to retrieve the skier, another boat drives over and cuts the line. The rules insist that you use a line of at least 21 m, but most skier's lines are 40–80 m in length. The faster you go, the longer the line you will need.

Ski handles are important too. They have got to be strong and comfortable. There are a few custom-made handles, which are made of nylon straps. These are the best type because they do not dig into your sides like the rope handles when 'wrapping'. 'Wrapping' is the style of skiing which is adopted by the skiers – the two handles are wrapped around your waist and held behind your back with one hand.

The arm which is free holds either a front handle or the line in front. If you prefer to use a handle, it should be positioned at about arm's length in front of you. Again, this will be personal preference, and in trying different ways you will find the most comfortable position. When using the line in front, it is best to make a knot for grip, in a position to suit yourself.

Next we come to the ski: this is the most important part of the skier's equipment, and the most expensive. Racers use a longer than normal mono ski. The usual length is about 6 ft 6 ins and the width is around 6.5 ins wide. The skis are flat and have a large fin at the rear. Most are made of wood, which makes them heavier and more stable at speed in rough water. Fibreglass skis are also available. The choice is wide, and the best way to select the ski is to find out which is more commonly used. If it is possible, borrow a few to try – this way you can find a ski which best suits you. When you have committed yourself to a ski, it must be kept in good condition. The bindings are also very important; again, there are a few different makes, so select the size and type you think will suit you. They too should be looked after carefully. The bindings should be positioned on the ski and firmly screwed down. The bindings should also be a firm fit – they should not be so tight that after a short time your feet go numb, and they should not be too loose so your feet move about. A regular check on the tightness and condition of the screws is most important for obvious reasons. The correct position of the bindings will depend on your size and weight. By speaking to the ski manufacturer, you will be able to get advice on the best position for you. The fin on the ski must again

be firmly screwed on, a check for rust along the welds of the fin must be made regularly and care must be taken not to damage or bend it. As I have stressed before, care must be taken with all your equipment. If you look after your gear, it will look after you. Regular checks on all your equipment for faults must be made, and if there are signs of wear, then the offending items must either be repaired or replaced at the earliest convenient time.

So, presuming you have a boat and crew, you are ready to tackle a ski race. To alleviate some of the pressure of pre-race nerves, it is best for the skier to concentrate on preparing him/herself and not get too involved in preparing the boat for launching. This should be done by the crew. Give yourself enough time before a race to sort out ski lines and lengths of ski lines to use. The length of line will depend on water conditions and what type of boat you are skiing behind. You will be the best judge of this, and experience will prove valuable in this preparation. The ski lines are best coiled in a bucket, or other similar container, so as not to get tangled in the boat when taking the line out at the start of the race. It is always best if you give yourself a few minutes in which to warm up and stretch your muscles before skiing. Some skiers choose to bind their ankles with tape – this is to give protection from the bindings where they might rub. It will also give you a certain amount of protection in the event of a fall, where it will help stop your ankles from twisting. Tape can also be used to make loose bindings tighter, but you must not tape your feet too tight, otherwise they will go numb and become painful. There are different methods in taping so it is best to watch other

skiers to find a way which will help you best. When you put your equipment on, make sure that everything fits comfortably and there are no loose ends which may break your concentration, e.g. a strap or buckle which flaps about while you are skiing can get annoying and take your mind off your skiing.

The start of the race is very important, in as much as if you miss the 'snatch' you will lose valuable ground on other competitors. Also, the driver must watch out for other boats and obstacles, as the starts can often become very congested. The start procedure is fairly simple: the 'start boat' will hold up two flags, which signals that there are three minutes before the start. In this time you will fit yourself into the ski and then sit on the edge of the boat ready for the start. In this time, make sure the ski is comfortable and that you have a firm grip on the line. After two and a half minutes, one flag will drop: this means there are just 30 seconds before the start. This is the time when the skier must get into the water and the line is taken

out. As soon as the line is tight, you must make sure you are ready for the start flag to drop. The driver must take care not to take the line out too fast, as he/she may 'snatch' the line from you. When the line is nearly out, the observer should tell the driver, so that he/she can slow down – 30 seconds is enough time to take the line out steadily and give the skier a short drag before the start flag goes down. There are two ways for the skier to start: the conventional way, with arms out in front, or already in the 'wrapped' position (the latter being more difficult, but more beneficial to a good start). When starting in the conventional way, you should have your knees bent in front of you with your arms straight, lean slightly forward, and when the boat pulls you out of the water, stand up. Just as the boat comes onto the plane, you will notice a slight cavitation, and a drop in speed. This is your chance to get 'wrapped' so pull on the handles – this should give you enough slack and time to achieve the 'wrapped' position. If you miss this chance, the driver will normally have to slow down a touch to give you another chance to get 'wrapped'. Some people prefer to start with their ski positioned in the middle of their ski handles. This will help to keep the ski in a straight line, but you must make sure that the 'v' is long enough so that when you are up it does not get caught under the front of your ski. When doing the 'wrapped' start, you must be proficient in starting the conventional way. When you drop into the water, adopt the position right away, so as to give you enough time to get comfortable. When the line is tight, bend your knees up in front of you, as in the normal way, and then lean back on the handles slightly. In this position, it will be possible for you

to be dragged quicker, enabling you to get a much faster start. When the boat pulls you out, pull up on your front arm and lean back a bit. Unlike the conventional start, as soon as you are standing, there will be no need for the driver to slow down, so you will already have an advantage over your competitors with a faster start. As I have said before, you should only attempt this start when you have become proficient at starting the normal way. Therefore, when the flag drops, and you are up and in a 'wrapped' position, the race is on. In the run to the first turn, you and your crew must watch all the other competitors, as it can become very dangerous and congested. In some races, it is possible to have as many as 50 or 60 boats in a race, with everyone jockeying for their best position. Sometimes the race organisers will include a long first lap – this will help to separate the field so as not to get too many boats hitting the first turn together. What you must remember is that this is the

first lap of many and any mistakes or falls here can end your challenge for the race. It is more important to be first across the finish line and not first on the start lap, so take this lap, and possibly the next two laps, getting settled, warmed up, and finding out the different types of water on the course. These few laps are important to some people for calming nerves and getting into the right frame of mind for the rest of the race. In these laps, you must also be aware of your competition and not let them get too far ahead of you, or it will be difficult to catch them. In some races, particularly the flat ones, you will probably not get a chance to settle in for too long, so you must learn to adjust quickly. When you are settled, you will be ready to speed the pace up, not forgetting you have a long way to go, so you must pace yourself so as not to get too tired too quickly.

When you have gained experience of racing with your

crew, you will find that racing becomes a tactical sport, with competitors playing a kind of cat and mouse game, with positions changing quite frequently. You will learn when to challenge people for their positions, and when not to challenge. When you are behind somebody, you will sometimes have the upper hand, in as much as you can see this skier and he/she cannot see you. The skier will often be told by his/her crew that you are close behind, and this will put him/her under a certain amount of pressure. This will give you an advantage – you must pick your best opportunity to challenge the leading skier for that position. You must be ready to race, because when you are alongside someone, the speed will noticeably increase, and then it comes down to skill, strength, determination, courage, and your will to win which will help you to pass. It is at this point – where you challenge for position and you are alongside another team of the same standard – that you will find out the mental pressures involved. You will find that your rival will not give his/her position up easily, and after a few laps of racing, both yourself and the other skier will be thinking that the other will slow down soon. Neither of you will, and after a few more laps you will be wondering how long you can keep this pace up for. This is where you will discover how much determination and will to win your opponent has, as well as yourself, because if neither of you give in then it will either be a close finish or one of you will suffer a fall. It will be the skier that not only believes in his crew, but in him/herself, who will come out on top.

When your crew have gained enough experience, they will be able to assist you in your battle to outwit your opponents. For instance, if you are behind someone, they can come alongside the skier just so he/she can see the nose of your boat out of the corner of the eye, and this will sometimes break your opponent's concentration, again giving you the advantage. What you must remember is that your opponent will be doing the same things to you, so you will have to learn to cope with these distractions yourself.

Very rarely, while you are skiing, will you ski in the middle of the boat wake. Normally, unless the water is really rough, there is one side of the wake which is slightly smoother, so you must use your judgment to ski in the best place. In your preparation it is sometimes better to ski from a ski pole; this will help to stop the ski line dipping into the water, particularly on turns where the line may sometimes go a bit slack when decreasing speed. When turning, you must remember not to go outside the wake, as this is against the rules and you can be penalised for it. When turning, your speed should come down slightly and the driver should hold a steady line through the turn. Concentrate on the water in front of you and be careful not to skip out, as this can cause problems. The boat driver, when coming out of the turn, must remember not to accelerate until the skier is also out of the turn. The observer will be telling the driver if the turn is being taken too tightly, again causing problems for the skier.

If you turn too wide or too slow you risk losing valuable distance. As you get better, you will be able to corner quicker and often be able to make ground on the opposition. Races can be won and lost on turns. For example, if you have the inside line while racing with someone, you have the advantage; your opponent will be working harder than you, and will need to take more risks to gain on you; you will not need to go quite so fast because the ground you may lose on the straights you can regain in the turns. In flat conditions, it is possible not to slow down for the turn – you will need to lean into the turn a bit more than usual and, because there will not be any big waves to tackle, you should have no problems about skipping out of the wake. When racing in rough waters, you must adjust your skiing position and style to cope with waves. If you are racing on the sea, you will sometimes find that the waves are a regular size and distance apart. This will help you to read the conditions, and after a few laps you will get used to it and will be expecting what each lap will be like. You will probably be able to ski better on one straight than perhaps others, so this is where you should make your moves on the opposition.

Sometimes you will find the water conditions irregular and the waves of no set size or pattern. This is where you must learn to use your judgement to read the conditions. You will find it easier maybe to jump over some waves and ski across others. This type of condition is difficult – not only for the skier, but for the crew as well. The driver and observer will sometimes find it difficult to read the conditions for you, so you will all have to feel your way round until you get familiar with the course. Some people find flat water easier to ski in. When you get up into the higher formulae, particularly formula 1, where the boat speed can often be in the eighties and possibly the nineties, you will not find it so easy. Your reactions will have to be very sharp to react to the conditions,

and you will also find the mental pressures are higher. The pull from the boat will be much greater, so you must be strong to pull back on the line to keep a constant style. When you start to become tired, be careful not to be pulled over the front of the ski, because this is normally the way in which you may fall. If you lean against the pull you will find it better, but you will also find it tiring on your legs. Your crew must react that much quicker to your needs and be much more aware of the other boats. When everything is at its limit, the smallest mistake or hesitation can often lead to a fall, or even boat problems, so you must all be physically and mentally very fit to cope with the high speeds.

All skiers will have a slightly different style, so you must find out which is your best position, where you are most comfortable, and achieve the best balance. Normally, it is advisable to hold the handles just below the small of your back and lean back slightly on the handles –

how far you lean back will depend on how fast you are going. Keep your knees bent and out in front of you – this will help stop you from being pulled over the front of your ski. Also, your legs will be able to take the shock of the waves without sending the jolts through your body, which will make you jump about. Think of your legs as car shock absorbers that do all the work over the water and give your body a smooth ride. Your front arm is also important: it will help you keep your balance, and you will be able to take out any jolts caused by slack line or big waves. To picture the stance, imagine someone skiing, and draw a line through the skier's waist. Above the line the skier should not be moving too much, but below the line his/her legs will be moving very quickly to adjust to the waves, and to give a better ride.

The skier must be generally fit, he/she must be strong in the legs and back where most of the stress will be. The skier must also have a lot of stamina. Each individual will have his/her own training programme which suits that skier: a general training programme will include strength, speed, reactions, stretching, endurance, and competition. For the strength, weight training is the best. You should seek professional help in this department as injuries can often occur if you are inexperienced. You must prepare your legs and get them used to fast movement. Ways to train for this include sprinting, running up stairs and running on the spot. This will familiarise your leg muscles to work quickly and increase blood and oxygen flow through them. You must have sharp reactions, so pick a fast sport like squash, for instance, where you will need fast reactions to play well. Squash is a good game to use as a training session

– it not only speeds your reactions, but makes your legs move fast, and it also helps you concentrate. If you play squash, try and play someone who is better than you – it will help you to improve, and also help you train to your maximum ability.

Suppleness is most important. You should stretch your muscles regularly to achieve a high range of mobility. This will help prevent you from pulling muscles in training and, in the event of a fall while skiing, it will give you a better chance of coming through without any injuries.

You must have plenty of stamina to last for a race. It is many a skier's downfall to weaken at the end of a race, and many good positions have been lost to stronger skiers, so you must work hard in this department. The best stamina builders are running and swimming. How successful you want to be in the sport will depend on how much determination, dedication, and support you get. You must train regularly and, whatever programme you set yourself, try to do it to the best of your ability and discipline yourself to work hard. Some people may find training a chore, so if there are friends you can train with, it will often make it easier, more enjoyable, and will give you some competition as well. There is no substitute for skiing. All other training will help but the more opportunity you get to ski the better for you it will be. When you are ski training, remember not to go too mad and have a fall, as you may injure yourself. I say this because skiers in the past have taken unnecessary risks and had bad falls in training. The amount of training you do will depend on the individual. If you feel you are weak in a particular department, then you must strengthen there.

Most of your training should be done out of season, over a period of time. The skier who starts training two weeks before the start will sometimes be too late in the preparation for major honours.

A few points to remember: ski racing is a team sport, where all three members of the team have an important role to play. Your equipment should be kept in first-class condition and that includes the boat. You should be physically fit and strong. You should have determination, dedication, discipline and the will to win, if you want to be successful. The more work you put in, the better results you will get. Success will not come overnight, so keep working hard – experience will tell in the end.

11 FREESTYLE SKIING

BY FOUR-TIME PRO TOUR CHAMPION, SCOTT CLACK

Scott Clack, a name synonymous with freestyle waterskiing, spends half his life in the air and much of that time upside down. When he is not performing spectacular aerial tricks in freestyle competitions, or flipping from the ramp in a show at Florida's world-famous Cypress Gardens, he is flying to tournaments and exhibitions. He has amazed crowds all over the world with his form of jumping. He not only jumps around 120 ft off the ramp, he also adds a few flips and twists. His repertoire includes a one-ski double-front flip, one-ski 720s (a 720-degree turn in the air), two-ski double-front flip, two-ski mobius (a full twisting back flip), one-ski gainer (back flip), and one-ski mobius (full twisting back flip). I wonder what his mother, Barbara Cooper Clack – the first woman to jump 100 ft – makes of her son's jumping. 'It's for the daredevils and crazy guys,' she once told her son. But it didn't stop him from learning one trick after another, although he admits he hated learning some of the one-ski tricks.

'Learning the one-ski tricks was so painful.I took so many falls, broke so many ribs. I broke the same rib four times one summer. I hated doing the one-ski front flip but I had to do it to win. So I kept practising it. Finally, I said, "forget it, I'll try to win without it". Occasionally, I would, but I needed to do it to win. Still, today, I hate the one-ski front flip. I've taken more falls and bruises from that than anything else.'

Freestyle skiing is as dangerous and as exciting as long-distance jumping. It has developed from an act in ski shows to a competitive discipline in its own right, with big cash prizes available on the American pro circuit.

The top freestylers can jump 130 ft on one ski – with a flip or two thrown in for good measure. Many skiers would be happy with that distance without also adding a front flip, twist or gainer. Unlike other events in waterskiing, style and form are important in freestyle jumping and the skier can score as many points for form as distance. Like trick skiing, the harder the manoeuvre, the more points it scores. Since the introduction of one-ski tricks in 1987, all freestyle tricks have had one- and two-ski versions, but with the one-ski jumps scoring much higher, because it is harder to keep your balance when landing on just one ski.

The great thing about this event is that it is constantly developing. Flips have become easy and common – now the top skiers are going for one-ski double-front flips and 540s, where you land with your back to the boat. But the key to these tricks is mastering the basics and getting a feel for the sport. Before you attempt to learn any freestyle manoeuvres, you should be an accomplished long-distance jumper. You should be competent at cutting to the ramp, maintaining a good position on your approach and on the ramp (back straight, leaning slightly forward, knees bent, head up, skis shoulder-width apart), and be able to get good lift off the ramp (you will have more time then to complete your trick). If you are a good jumper, the next step is to learn the manoeuvres away from the ramp. You have to know in your mind what you have to do and then practise – either on a

trampoline, in a swimming pool or off the side of a dock. Flipping into deep water from a dock will help your body and mind become aware of the feeling and teach you to sense where the water is for landing.

Have a friend simulate the boat's pull. When I'm learning a new trick I like to take it easy. I slow the boat down from about 35 to 30 m.p.h. And I use shorter skis, like an old pair of jumpers that I've cut down. Make the bindings so they are loose and will come off easily if something goes wrong.

Here are three basic freestyle manoeuvres.

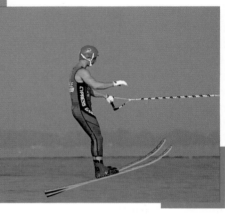

HELICOPTER 360°

Set up: start with a ramp height of 5.5 ft and a boat speed of approximately 30 m.p.h. The boat path should be between the ramp and the 45 ft (inside) buoy.

1 'Wrap' the rope behind your back, placing the handle at the small of your back. Hold the handle in place with your left hand. Place your right hand slightly in front of your right hip and grasp the tow rope.

2 Bend knees, keep head up and weight slightly on the balls of your feet.

3 Approach the ramp the same as a basic rideover, aiming towards the centre of the ramp.

4 Prepare for take-off. As you reach the top of the ramp, start the turn with the right hip, pushing down on the rope slightly with the right hand, initiating the spin.

5 The spin. Starting the turn with the right hip, and keeping the handle at the small of the back and head up helps ensure the correct axis.

6 The finish. Upon completion of the spin, push the left hand down slightly and re-grab the handle with the right hand.

FLIP

Once again, approach the ramp in the same way as a rideover. Line up with the centre of the ramp – the boat speed should be about 32 m.p.h. and the path should be the same as for the helicopter.

1 Keep head up and bend knees slightly. Keep weight slightly on the balls of your feet.

2 Take off. When you reach the top of the ramp, keep your shoulders square with the top of it. Springing upward and pulling the rope to your waist will start the rotation. Next, roll your shoulders and head down. Bring your chest (down) towards your knees. Do not bring knees up to chest.

3 The finish. Finish by spotting the water between your skis as you complete the rotation. As you see the water, open up to stop the rotation.

To ensure proper rotation lead slightly with left shoulder on take off.

Note: Spins and turns are accelerated by tucking, by bringing the arms and legs in. If you over-rotate, extend your arms.

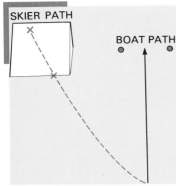

Take off

110

GAINER

(Back flip)

The boat should be driven at approximately 34 m.p.h. along a path just inside the 45 ft (inside) buoy.

1 The approach. The approach is a progressive double wake cut, starting slow and building the speed as you cut to the ramp. Once again, the head is up, knees bent and your weight slightly on the balls of your feet.

2 Edging. Edging into the ramp is one of the most important things to remember. Doing this keeps the rope tight – this will help during the rotation.

3 Diagram. As you reach the top of the ramp, spring upward, pushing up with your hips and, at the same time, push your head up and back.

Important: Do not bend your knees and sit back. Starting the trick early could result in hitting your head on the ramp. It is very important to spring up *and* back – not just backwards. On the first couple of attempts, drop the rope at the base of the ramp, but continue to do the trick as if you had the rope in your hands.

EQUIPMENT

Jump skis, helmet, flotation vest or wetsuit with built-in flotation, pylon-mounted rope for quick release.

Don't try these stunts without an experienced driver and a release operator who knows what he/she is doing.

BECOMING A CHAMPION *12*

BY FOUR-TIMES WORLD CHAMPION, SAMMY DUVALL

Sammy Duvall was lying in fourth place overall at the 20th World Water Ski Championship, with just his three jumps to go in the competition.

Sammy Duvall with the proof that he has got 'It'.

He was under tremendous pressure. As the leader in the jump event, he was the last skier out on the water. Mike Hazelwood had just jumped 192 ft to increase the pressure on the 5 ft 8 in skiing star, who had picked up his first world overall title on the same site, Thorpe Park, England, six years earlier. Duvall knew he had to jump 58 m (190 ft) to win the jump gold and 59.7 m (196 ft) to retain his overall crown.

His first effort was 59.2 m (194 ft). The jump gold was his. Could he go even further and deprive the brilliant Mick Neville of the overall title again? Duvall went wide, cut late, got a great spring, flew through the air and landed softly – 200 ft, a new championship record. It was one of the most dramatic moments in the sport's history and it gave Duvall the overall title once more, his fourth on the trot, another record achievement.

Afterwards, he said 'I wasn't going to ski in these championships, but when people started saying I couldn't do it again, I knew I had to prove I could . . . I reached deep inside myself and pulled out that jump.'

It goes to show what can be done if you have the will to win and get in the right frame of mind for an event. At all levels in waterskiing, being mentally and physically prepared can make all the difference between being a loser and a champion.

One of the most important things I have learned over the years of competitive skiing is that winning once or twice is easy, but to win consistently over a season is much more difficult. Why? My best conclusion consists of two parts: physical ability and mental toughness. Which is more important? Mental toughness, without question. Obviously, it takes a combination of both to be a winner, but at the professional level of waterskiing, mental toughness is about 95 per cent of winning.

I'll try to explain to you how the winning combination, which works for me, can also work for you at any level of athletic competition. First of all, the mental or psychological side of winning. Over the years I have been fortunate to meet many top athletes from various sports. Some of them were good at what they do, others were great! It is very easy to spot a winner by the look in his eye. It is a look of drive, determination, of . . . 'I refuse to lose'. It is the look of IT! What is IT? That is a tough question but I

offer this definition. IT (defined) is the ability to reach inside oneself, regardless of the situation, and to pull out from oneselves what it takes to make a winning performance. I truly believe IT is what has kept me at the top of my sport for so long. Now I'll try to explain how you get IT and use IT to reach your goals.

GOALS

Sports are no different to life when it comes to goals. You must have goals to take you from one level to the next for the betterment of your sport, your life and your job. Without goals we're lost, meandering through life – operating at half-speed, with no control over our own destiny. You must set goals, and then lay a straight path from point A to point B to achieve them. If you deviate along that path, it will make it that much more difficult to achieve what you really want. I learned at a very young age what goals were all about. My sister Camille and I were fortunate to have a great set of parents, who taught us what goals were. As we became better skiers, our father wanted us to try harder. This is the way his programme worked. At the beginning of the skiing season, we sat down and wrote out our goals for the season. No one knew what was on each other's paper. We then stuffed them into an envelope. My father would then take a $100 bill, tear it in half, put half in the envelope and seal it and put the other half in his wallet. At the end of the season, we would tear open the envelopes and if we reached our goals, we received the other half of the $100. I was eleven years old then and I still stop and take time to write down my goals in skiing, in business, and in life, before my season begins. I also believe it is important to write them down,

not just to think them. Seeing your goals will spur you on to reach them.

I have explained goals but obviously there's more to winning than just goals. You also need:

Determination – you must have the will and ambition to be the best you can possibly be.
Sacrifice – you must be willing to sacrifice those things that are most important to you to achieve your goals.
Discipline – the ability to go out and train, regardless of the conditions or how you feel. Discipline goes hand in hand with sacrifice.
Dedication – you must be totally dedicated and truly believe in what you are trying to achieve.
Motivation – you must be able to motivate yourself to reach your goals.

All of these things make up IT, and by possessing IT, you will become a winner.

Sammy Duvall on his way to clinching his third world crown.
Top: *with his sister, Camille.*

113

PHYSICAL TRAINING

Almost as important is being in top physical condition. All serious skiers should use a strengthening programme, not only to help raise their overall level of skiing, but also to improve their physical well-being.

First of all, there is one important point that should be made. To improve your skiing, you've got to be strong and flexible. Therefore, in addition to training with weights, you have to develop a programme to increase your flexibility. Free weight training will tend to make your muscles tighten and become shorter and fatter, decreasing your flexibility. I suggest you take aerobic classes or spend a good deal of time cycling. Aerobics and cycling will vastly improve your flexibility and stamina, so that you may ski longer with less effort. For example, when I began free weight lifting, I noticed that I began to bulk up and put on weight but I also lost a great deal of flexibility. I immediately began aerobic classes and gained more

flexibility than I ever dreamed of having. The end result is a much stronger Sammy Duvall, and, most importantly, as my weight dropped (due to aerobics) my strength per pound (total body weight) increased.

So, here is my workout. (Understand that you can train much harder during the off-season than when you are skiing.)

● Monday/Wednesday/Friday – weight training.
● Tuesday/Thursday/Saturday – aerobics or cycling.
● Sunday – rest.

Most skiers tend to use their legs and back muscles more than their upper bodies. Both are important, of course, but I feel that having a strong back and legs will aid you the most in the long run. Please note you should increase your weights with each set.

Monday (in order):

1 Stretching and warm up.

2 Leg extensions – three sets.

3 Leg curls – three sets.

Cycling is good for skiers.

If you find weight training easy, you aren't lifting enough weight.

4 Power squats – five to six sets.

5 Incline leg press – three to four sets.

6 Calf raises – three sets with weight.

7 Sit ups/crunches/stomach exercises.

Note: A set consists of 10–12 repetitions (reps). As weight increases, reps should decrease. If you find this too easy, you aren't lifting enough weight.

Tuesday: Aerobic class, one hour minimum, plus stationary bike or real bicycling if possible.

Wednesday:

1 Stretching – warm up.

2 Bench press – three sets.

3 Flys – three sets.

4 Pull over – three sets.

5 Pull downs (behind neck) – three sets.

6 Pull down (chest) – three sets.

7* Preacher curls – three sets (narrow grip).

8* Preacher curls – three sets (wide grip).

9* Tricep press – three sets (wide grip).

10 Dumbbell curls – each arm until failure.

11 Stomach exercises and jump rope.

*Alternate 7-8-9 curl-tricep press curl until set is complete.

Thursday: Aerobic class, minimum one hour, and bicycling, if possible.

Friday: Repeat Monday's workout.

Saturday: Aerobic class, minimum one hour.

Sunday: Rest and prepare for next week.

There are a few important factors to note:

1 If you do not wish to build muscle mass, do not increase your weight each set, but do higher reps, 20–25 per set. This is often the case with women.

2 No workout is set in stone. Work with the above information and curtail it to meet your needs.

3 Understand that during your skiing season you must cut back on your training programme in order to maintain more energy for your skiing. However, do not quit totally. I recommend weights at least one day a week, and aerobics two days a week, to maintain flexibility. If you put this programme to use, I guarantee you will see an improvement in your skiing ability.

WINNING PERFORMANCES

I have been known for many years as a skier who produces the winning performances when the pressure is really on. Much of that ability has come with competitive experience. I believe the finest example of this was my performance at the World Championships in London, England, September 1987.

Cut back workouts in the season to save your energy for skiing.

115

The right preparation mentally and physically helps Sammy produce the right performance at the right time.

The chips were down and it really looked as if I would not go on to win my fourth consecutive world overall title. I could see it in people's eyes. My friends, my competitors, my enemies – all thought that it was over. I even believe my family had their doubts. But as I began my walk to the starting dock, my wife Sue said: 'I know it looks impossible, but if anyone can do it you can, you're the champion.' That reconfirmed what I was truly feeling deep down inside. *I could do it!* The minute my feet hit the water, I felt that nothing could stand in my way. I had slalomed and tricked poorly throughout the competition and the only way for me to win the overall was to put together a jump of around 197 ft, only 2.5 ft shy of my personal best. I led jumping after the first round, so I was seeded last. As I waited my turn on the starting jetty, it began to seem more impossible as good jumpers like Geoff Carrington, Carl Roberge, and Glenn Thurlow all seemed to have difficulty breaking the 190 ft mark. Then, Mike Hazelwood popped off a nice one in the low 190s to take the lead. At that time, Mike's father, Maurice, had an argument with my sister, Camille, and me. He was probably trying to disrupt my thought process. It was the biggest mistake he could

have made, as it got me more fired up to win, and to take the championships. When I reached the end of the lagoon at Thorpe Park, preparing for my first jump, I took all of the pressure of the day along with Maurice Hazelwood's words and converted them into energy. When I landed my first jump, I knew it was enough to take the jumping championship, but I wanted more for the overall title. As the boat towed me past the jetty, my family cheered me on and I could tell by the atmosphere of my competitors that they, too, believed I could accomplish my goal.

When I turned to go to the ramp on my second jump, I knew right then that it would be the one. I would later tell my family, which includes my good friends Jack and Lelani Travers, that it was the most perfect jump I have ever had in my entire career. I truly believe that you may only have two to three jumps that perfect in practice, tournaments, at any point in your life, and that was one of them. I won the overall title for the fourth consecutive time.

How did I accomplish this? Because I had IT! Having IT will make you a winner and champion. Throughout this chapter I have tried to explain what IT is and give you examples of how I have used IT to win. Regardless of what level of skiing you are trying to achieve, being goal-oriented will help you to be a better competitor and to be a winner. Take the time to analyse yourself and check to see if you possess the six points I mentioned: goals, determination, sacrifice, discipline, dedication, and motivation. If you push yourself to expand on them, plus have a good physical training programme, who knows, you may be the next champion of tomorrow. Go for it!

Up to old tricks in the 1985 Worlds in France.

3

WATERSKIING
FOR EVERYONE

13 BOAT DRIVING

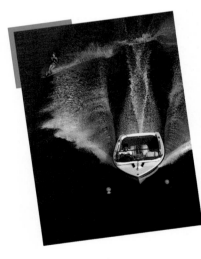

Whatever mistake a skier makes, it is always the boat driver's fault – whether it is really, or it isn't. Always be prepared to be blamed for everything and remember, a bad boat driver can spoil a skiing session or, worse, make it dangerous. So, it is important that the boat driver knows what he or she is doing. You should:

- Know your boat. You should be able to operate it blindfold. Get the feel for it without a skier. Practise docking, using a buoy as a make-believe dock. Try doing it without relying on reverse, your brake.

- Know your skier's capabilities, and adjust your speed accordingly.

- Know the area, the restrictions, etc., in your lake/river, where the jetty is, the landing procedure peculiar to that area, where the shallow water is, where there are submerged obstacles, etc., the local speed restrictions, the currents, etc.

- Know your sport. It helps if you are an experienced skier.

- Know the safety code. You should always have an observer on board who will be able to relay signals from the skier. All three of you must know the standard hand signals and any others appropriate to your situation. Before you set off, you must make sure your boat is fully equipped – that it has a lifejacket for each person on board, a bailer and a paddle, a fire extinguisher and anchor, a good rear-view mirror and plenty of fuel.

At the start of a skiing session, make sure the skier has all the right equipment, e.g. lifejacket, suitable skis for the skier's size, ability and type of skiing he/she aims to do, and a helmet if jumping. Before you set off, make sure you have an unrestricted view ahead of you. Also, make sure you can see all the towline, from the ski pole to the handle. For a deepwater start, make sure the skier has the tips of his skis out of the water and is holding the handle with both hands. For beach and dock starts, make sure you can see the coiled rope clearly and that any loops of slack that the skier may have taken are thrown away before you open the throttle.

While the skier is getting into the correct starting position, practise putting the boat in and out of forward gear. Very slowly move forward taking the slack out of the line, so it becomes taut. When the skier shouts 'Hit it', accelerate smoothly so the boat gently pulls the skier out.

There will be less drag once the boat is planing and the skier is up, so ease back on the throttle to the correct speed for the skier's size – for children, that will be 15–20 m.p.h., for adults, 20–24 m.p.h. is usually enough when they are beginners (increasing the speed as they progress, by a couple of miles when they come to drop a ski), 24–28 for the average slalom skier, going up to 34–36 for the more experienced skier. If the skier is ploughing through the water, you are going too slow. Increase your speed until the skier is gliding through the water with little effort. Constantly check your rear-view mirror, so you know where the skier is.

You can help beginners and recreational skiers by easing back the throttle a little if they look like falling. But it is most important that any speed changes are gradual, so you don't jerk the skier off balance. When the skier falls, your observer should call 'Fall'. The driver should then close the throttle, turn and 'idle back' for the skier, if he has signalled OK (clasped hands above the head). Going slowly is not only safer but also creates less disturbance to the course. Approach the fallen skier on the driver's side, so you can see the skier and won't hit him/her. Also, approach so that the wind and/or current will take the boat away from the skier, not push the boat on to him/her. Always be aware of the towline – don't run or back over it. If the skier wants to continue, slowly go past so that he/she can swim to, or reach out for, the handle, and get set for another deepwater start (see diagrams below). If a fallen skier has not signalled OK, return to him/her as quickly as possible.

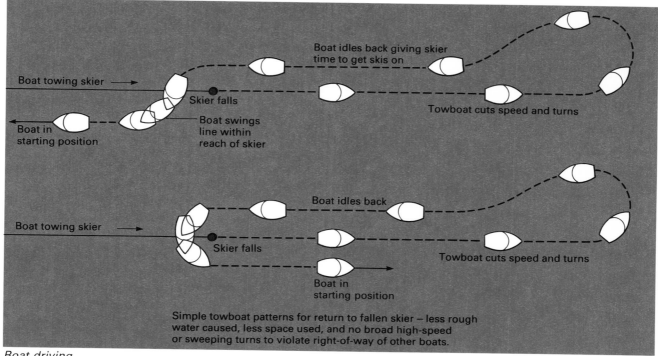

Boat driving

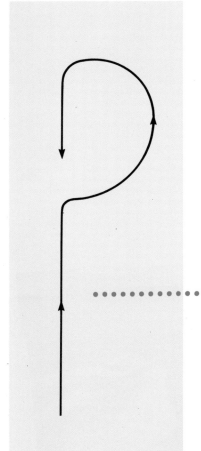

Turns should be gradual, wide arcs

Always shut down the engine before you take a skier on board, and always drive from the driver's seat. If you sit on the side, you can easily fall in while the boat carries on. Likewise, passengers should always sit *in* the boat. Drive smoothly and in a straight line, well away from swimmers, canoeists, sailboats, fellow skiers and other water users. Turns should be gradual, wide arcs. When you are turning, think of the letter P (see diagram left). This will give the skier longer to set up for the course. Always check the skier's position before turning – this should be directly behind the boat. Don't turn towards the skier.

Go up and down the same course to minimise water disturbance. When the session is over, approach the landing area slowly and parallel to it, so when the skier lets go, he/she will sink quickly well away from anything which cause injury.

DRIVING FOR DIFFERENT SKIERS

BEGINNERS

A driver can help learners by easing off the throttle when they look like falling, and the driver can help them turn. Signal your turn in good time and be aware of where the skier is. He/she should be between the wakes when you turn. If the skier gets caught inside the turn, he/she will sink, so open up the throttle. If the beginner gets caught outside the wake, the skier will be thrown out on the whip, so ease back on the throttle until you have turned and then accelerate before the beginner gets caught with too much slack.

SLALOM

Drive in a straight line down the centre of the boat buoys, maintaining the correct speed throughout. Sounds easy, doesn't it? The problem is that the skier will be pulling the boat from side to side as he/she turns from buoy to buoy, and pulling down the speed when crossing the wakes. The design of boat can help the driver to maintain the correct line. If the boat is heavy, has fins fitted to the keel and a centrally mounted ski pole, it will be harder for the skier to pull if off course.

So, the driver has to lightly compensate for the skier by gently using the throttle and steering wheel. But don't try to steer the boat through the course – aim it in a straight line. You have to learn to anticipate the skier's pull and increase revs accordingly before the speed drops, and to pull back the throttle before the speed increase shows on the speedometer. If any change shows on the speedometer, it is too late – the skier will feel the surge, or drop in power. The skier should not notice any changes in direction or speed.

After leaving the course, continue in a straight line until the skier is directly behind the boat again, then make your nice wide turn. If the skier is up to the higher speeds, slow down outside the course to give him/her a breather.

TRICKS

Concentrate on driving in a straight line (use a landmark to help you) and at a constant speed (the one specified by the skier). The speed is likely to be between 14–20 m.p.h. Use the throttle gently to compensate for the skier's pulls (e.g. heavy landings from wake tricks). Make sure the weight in the boat is evenly distributed so that the wakes are the same shape and size.

JUMPING

Stick to the line the skier has specified (e.g. the distance from the 15 m buoy) and maintain the right speed by correcting it constantly as the skier pulls wide for the counter-cut. Then, anticipate the counter-cut by applying more power, ease off as the skier coasts wide to your right, maintain line and speed as you wait for the cut. Anticipate this and compensate for the skier's strength. When the skier launches into the air you will feel a surge of power, so ease back and get the speed under control again. Don't turn until the skier is past the rideout buoy. Be aware and alert – jumping is the most dangerous discipline.

SLALOM TIMES – Times to 1/100th of a second

Speed kph	Full course			3rd buoy		
	Fast	Actual	Slow	Fast	Actual	Slow
58	15.93	16.08	16.23	6.65	6.77	6.88
55	16.75	16.95	17.15	7.01	7.13	7.27
52	17.59	17.93	18.28	7.40	7.55	7.69
49	18.65	19.03	19.43	7.85	8.01	8.18
46	19.84	20.27	20.72	8.35	8.53	8.72
43	21.19	21.68	22.20	8.92	9.13	9.34
40	22.74	23.31	23.91	9.57	9.81	10.06
37	24.54	25.20	25.90	10.33	10.61	10.90
34	26.64	27.42	28.25	11.21	11.54	11.89

JUMP TIMES

	kph	82 metres				41 metres			
		slow	act.	fast	tol. +/−	slow	act.	fast	tol. +/−
Men, Men 2, Senior 1 Men	57	5.28	5.18	5.08	.10	2.66	2.59	2.52	.07
Senior 2 Men	54	5.62	5.47	5.32	.15	2.83	2.73	2.63	.10
Junior Girls Ladies Junior Boys Senior 1 Ladies Senior 3 Men	51	5.89	5.79	5.69	.10	2.97	2.89	2.81	.08
Senior 2 and 3 Ladies Dauphin Boys	48	6.30	6.15	6.00	.15	3.18	3.08	2.98	.10
Dauphin Girls	45	6.76	6.56	6.36	.20	3.43	3.28	3.13	.15
	42	7.23	7.03	6.83	.20	3.66	3.51	3.36	.15
	39	7.77	7.57	7.37	.20	3.93	3.78	3.63	.15

BAREFOOT
As above, it is crucial to maintain a straight line and the correct speed.

RACING
Be aware of other boats and skiers. Never drive behind or too close to a skier.

Most boating accidents are alcohol or drugs related, so never get into a boat if you are intoxicated. And remember, most safety rules are common sense – so use what's between your ears and think of other water users.

HAND SIGNALS

Skiers, drivers and observers should know the standard hand signals.

1 Thumb up – faster.

2 Thumb down – slower.

3 Slashing motion across throat – cut engine/stop.

4 Circular motion of index finger over head – about to turn.

5 Pat on head – return to dock.

6 Making an O with thumb and index finger – OK (e.g. speed is OK).

7 Clasping hands over head while in the water – I'm OK (after falling).

ANYONE CAN SKI

14

BY ROBIN NICHOLS, THE BRITISH DISABLED WATER SKI ASSOCIATION'S CHIEF COACH

Above   *Alan Pettigred, paraplegic.*
Left   *John Ramm, leg amputee.*

Waterskiing is a sport for all. Men and women, young and old – and virtually all classes of physical disability – can benefit from waterskiing.

Those who are blind, deaf, have lost arms or legs, and many who can only normally get about in wheelchairs, can enjoy this sport. There are also a great many mentally handicapped people who can be taught to waterski, if patience and understanding are used fully and the risks understood. Some organisations, notably in America, have specialised in providing water rides on various board devices for mentally handicapped people. In all cases, the aim is to integrate the disabled into the normal ski world, where they can enjoy the sport among able-bodied friends without special assistance.

The history of the first pioneers of disabled waterskiing is not well defined, but there are fragmented press accounts of disabled waterskiers all over the world from about 1950. Most of these were amputees or blind and, as with the development of ordinary waterskiing, the first attempts took place in Canada, America, Australia, or Europe. In Great Britain, the first formal organisations got under way on July 1 1978, when the late David Nations brought together all those interested at the Ruislip Water Ski Club. Subsequently, the British Disabled Water Ski Association was formed by its first chairman, Tony Edge, a wartime leg amputee, who lived just long enough to see the Association establish its own training centre at Heron Lake, Wraysbury, in 1983. At this time, groups of disabled skiers also established themselves in Belgium, Norway, Canada, and America. Since then, there has been a great growth in numbers and skill, and the first world championships for the disabled, the First World Trophy for Disabled Water Skiers, took place at Heron Lake in July 1987. Disabled waterskiers form a part of the International Water Ski Federation.

Anyone with at least three sound limbs can waterski normally. For leg amputees, this usually means learning to ski on one leg, since the use of artificial limbs has, in most cases, proved to be a hindrance to learning. For those with only one usable arm, the learning process is helped by use of the 'Delger' sling, named after the British Water Ski Federation's coach Ray Delger, who first introduced this simple and effective aid. Australia's astounding one-arm athlete Geoff Burgess, with regular 35-metre leaps from the ski jump, has proved that such an aid is not vital to advanced waterskiing.

For more complicated limb disabilities, such as the loss of two limbs or partial paralysis of one side as sometimes happens after a stroke, the question of using waterskis is one that needs individual assessment by an experienced instructor. What is clear, however, is that such people should first obtain experience of fast movement over water on some form of ski board. Blind and deaf people can ski normally but the learning process can be greatly speeded up by experienced instructors. For wheelchair users, which includes all kinds of spinal paralysis, multiple amputations, birth defects, nerve and muscle disorders, and the vast variety of disabilities from accident and disease, the way to waterski will be on some form of ski board.

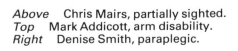

Above   Chris Mairs, partially sighted.
Top   Mark Addicott, arm disability.
Right   Denise Smith, paraplegic.

New techniques and ways of teaching disabled people to ski are being developed every year. Individuals all over the world have worked out their own methods but the only place that specialises solely in teaching disabled people to waterski is the Tony Edge Centre at Heron Lake. Here it has been found that the most rapid way of teaching disabled people to use one or two skis is to start on the Edge Triple Bar, designed by Tony Edge in 1980. This is a metal bar, two metres long, which can separate into three individual handles. A disabled pupil starts with an able-bodied instructor on either side. Once they are up and skiing, the instructor is alongside to give assistance and confidence. The bar is separated into individual handles as soon as the pupil is skiing correctly. Subsequently, the pupil learns to start with just one instructor, and finally on his own. Use of the Edge Triple Bar, which is made of stainless steel and aluminium, requires a tournament type inboard ski boat, or one that has the equivalent initial pulling power.

The next best method of teaching disabled beginners is with a boom on the side of a boat. These booms are widely available and commonly used for barefoot training. Although they are very efficient for teaching new skills to proficient skiers, many disabled skiers are quite apprehensive about being close to the boat, its spray and the unseen propeller. Additionally, the firm support of the bar must be exchanged for a rope and handle at some stage. The difference with an Edge Triple Bar is that progress is more rapid. The instructor is alongside to give confidence – and can quickly get the pupil into the correct skiing stance and then separate the handles – but can still give a hand

Roy Bassey, leg amputee, learns on the Edge Triple Bar with the help of instructors Robin Nichols and Marian Edge.

to stabilise balance, if necessary. Frequently, this will all take place during the first lesson. Solo skiing by one-legged, one-armed and blind pupils have all been achieved within three ski lessons, although progress naturally varies with individuals.

Blind skiers have been among the first and keenest disabled waterskiers, and their instruction can be the same as for able-bodied beginners – although an Edge Triple Bar will speed up the learning. What most blind people really appreciate is taking part in a sport without a guide in close proximity telling them where to go. This is perfectly safe in waterskiing where there are no obstructions. There are internationally accepted sound signals for communications, which briefly are:

- One horn or whistle blast, meaning it is safe to ski outside the wake of the boat.

- Two blasts, meaning the skier should get back and stay in the centre of the boat wake.

- One long blast, meaning 'let go of the handle'.

Above   Cancer victim Debbie Simms.
Left   Leg amputee Steve Woodcock on a kneeboard.

Ski board devices for all those unable to use one or two skis are the subject of much development, as could readily be seen from the variety of devices seen at the First World Trophy for Disabled Water Skiers. Currently most success in the United Kingdom is obtained by putting pupils initially on a fibreglass board called a 'Root 5' made by Valley Canoe Products and originally designed for surf canoeing on the Cornish coast. For the first run, an instructor goes alongside on a similar board, with his own ski rope and handle. These boards float in a stable manner, are easily manoeuvred and can be fitted with additional back support.

They should always be used with a canoeing or hockey type helmet, because when skiers roll out of them at slow speeds, the board may come down on their heads. A pupil may wish to progress to boards which are harder to start on but which can turn more tightly, such as the Sitz Ski originally developed by Frank Jaspers in Belgium, or the Kan Ski developed in America. Kneeboards are used by all types of disabled people and enable them to use a ski jump or learn the elements of trick skiing. They are particularly useful when only a low powered boat is available.

All disabled waterskiing must be done with ropes fixed through a quick release that can be operated by the observer in the tow boat. This really is logical when you think of the consequences of a blind skier misunderstanding a sound signal, a rope wrapped around a limb, or the failure of equipment. Wet or drysuits are essential for disabled beginners because they usually feel the cold more and are apt to spend more time in the water when learning.

In this sport, disabled athletes have followed the path of their able-bodied colleagues with trick, jump and slalom competitions, run under IWSF rules especially written for disabled waterskiing, so that different disability classes are subdivided equitably. Blind skiers replace the slalom event with wake crossing, where they have to cross the wake as many times as possible within a 15-second run. They also go over full-size ski jumps, using a guide to establish them in the correct position before carrying on alone over the jump. Board skiers use an inner slalom course, where the buoys are set 6.4 m from the centre of a standard length slalom course.

Disabled waterskiers with at least three limbs – and the blind – regularly barefoot, and in 1985, Mark Addicott (with only one usable arm), achieved fourth place in the British National Barefoot Championships novice class, competing against able-bodied skiers. Many records have been set by disabled waterskiers. Blind skiers Gerald Price and Nigel Verbeek crossed the English Channel on August 23 1981. In 1987 one-legged Steve Butterworth crossed the channel in 1 hour 34 minutes. Also in 1987, one-legged Wendy Mason skied around the Isle of Wight in 3 hours 31 minutes.

Standards will undoubtedly go up. At the moment, the best blind jumpers – such as Dave Hurst – have recorded distances of 18 metres. Trick skiing by the blind has enormous potential to increase above the 360 points scored by Sheila Holzworth, a member of the American team at the First World Trophy for Disabled Water Skiers. At this event, a leg amputee slalom record was set when Australian Len Sheppard skied around 3 buoys at 46 k.p.h. on an 18.25 m line. Regulations for speed records by the disabled are not yet established at a world level but Wendy Mason did ski over a measured 1 km on Lake Windermere at 46.68 m.p.h in October 1985, on one leg. It is still early days for this sport and we can expect to see many of these records eclipsed.

Above *Totally blind Dave Hurst jumping.*
Below *Leg amputee Wendy Mason barefoots.*
Bottom *Wendy Mason, Chris Mairs, Geoff King, Mark Addicott and Denise Smith training at the Tony Edge Centre.*

127

APPENDIX

RULES FOR SAFE WATERSKIING

Waterskiers

DO be a good swimmer and always wear a life jacket.

DO check your equipment always, e.g. wing nuts, loose binding, splinters and sharp metal.

DO understand and use approved signals between skier and observer and driver.

DO keep clear of solid obstacles – jetty, boats, mooring buoys, rocks, banks etc.

DO watch the water ahead of you at all times.

DO avoid falling forward – sit down, or if falling sideways, curl yourself into a ball.

DO always throw away the handle on falling.

DO come in slowly to land and run parallel to shore.

DO hold up your hand or ski to signal all is well after falling.

DO use an approved life jacket when jumping.

DO recover skis quickly, they will assist you to keep afloat.

DO NOT shout 'Hit it' to the driver until rope is taut and your ski tips are up.

DO NOT wrap rope around any part of the body (fingers, hands or foot)

DO NOT place any part of the body through the bridge (neck, arm or leg)

DO NOT ski in shallow water.

DO NOT ski at night.

DO NOT ski directly ahead of, or to the side of another boat.

DO NOT attempt fast landing directly towards the shore – sit down if coming in too fast.

DO NOT ski in unknown waters.

DO NOT jump from a boat whilst it is moving.

Ski boat driver

DO have a competent observer at all times in the boat watching the skier.

DO make sure observer understands water ski signals.

DO wait for the skier's signal and his ski tips above the water before starting.

DO give him a smooth and steady pull on take-off.

DO steer clear of other boats and floating obstacles.

DO shut off your motor before taking aboard a skier.

DO return immediately to pick up the skier.

DO always carry an extra life-jacket in the boat.

DO NOT turn sharply and put the skier in the water, gradual wide arc turns are the rule.

DO NOT take the skier aboard without shutting off the engine first.

DO NOT drive the boat through swimming or restricted areas.

DO NOT operate boat sitting on the side, sit in the seat.

First aid

It is strongly recommended that all participants in waterskiing (Instructors, Club Coaches, Drivers, Observers and skiers) are fully conversant in all methods of resuscitation and general first aid.

Note

It is strongly recommended that all participants in water ski JUMPING wear rubber jumping shorts. If these are not worn serious personal injury could result. Learners are recommended to wear two pairs of jumping shorts.